Are You A High Performing Coach?

Strategies For An Outstanding Sports Coaching Career

Caroline Gossage

An Amano Publishing Book
www.amanopublishing.com
First published in Great Britain in 2013 by Amano Publishing The information in this book is meant to supplement, not replace, proper sports coach training. Like any sports coaching involving speed, equipment, balance and environmental factors, sports coaching pose some inherent risk. The authors and publisher advise readers to take full responsibility for their safety and know their limits. Before practicing the skills described in this book, be sure that your equipment is well maintained, and do not take risks beyond your level of experience, aptitude, training, and comfort level.

Cover design © Michael Gossage, 2013
Book design and layout by Clark Kenyon, Camp Pope Publishing
Editing by Kim Kimber
Copyright © 2013 by Caroline Gossage
The right of Caroline Gossage to be identified as the author of this work has been asserted in accordance with Copyright, Designs and Patents Act, 1988.
ISBN: 978-0-9926661-0-1

No part of this book may be reproduced in any written, electronic, recording, or photocopying without written permission of the publisher or author. The exception would be in the case of brief quotations embodied in the critical articles or reviews and pages where permission is specifically granted by the publisher or author.

Although every precaution has been taken to verify the accuracy of the information contained herein, the author and publisher assume no responsibility for any errors or omissions. No liability is assumed for damages that may result from the use of information contained within.

Dedication

This book is dedicated to my son Michael.

Contents

About This Book 7

Introduction 8

Chapter 1: What Does Being A Coach Mean? 12

Chapter 2: Excellent Coaches Build Outstanding Coaching
    Programmes 19

Chapter 3: Skills Every Coach Should Have 32

Chapter 4: Communication 41

Chapter 5 : Stop, Look And Listen 56

Chapter 6: Long Term Self Development 69

Chapter 7: Managing The Body And The Mind 75

Chapter 8: Business And Career Management 82

Chapter 9: Money Management 87

Chapter 10: Injury Prevention and Health Management 91

Chapter 11: Why Should Coaches Practice What They Preach? ... 98

Chapter 12: Current Trends In The Coaching Industry–The New Way
    And Reality 107

Chapter 13: How To Be A Creative And Innovative Coach 115

Six Key Elements to Being A Great Coach 126

Acknowledgments 128

About The Author 129

Look To Learn From The Past In Order To Face The Future. Learning Never Stops.

About This Book

When I decided to write this book, it was out of sheer frustration in not being able to find what I was looking for. I wanted to identify what it was I needed in order to keep doing coaching right and what I could do to distinguish myself from all the other coaches. What did I need to do to excel as a coach? It is one thing to know how to develop athletes and quite another to develop coaches. How do you determine if the coach is mentally fit? How does a coach increase his/her creativity and performance? How does a coach hone their coaching style? How do they develop the unmeasureables such as, integrity, positive mental attitude, self-discipline, resilience, confidence, competitive spirit and all the other 112 positive attributes that I believe every coach looking to excel should have in place? This I finally figured out was what was missing in all the training and courses and studies I had taken up to this point. The training was focused on how to coach the player on the techniques and tactics and mental skills to become a good player. What physical exercises to do and how to improve fitness levels in the player, as required by the sport. Our sport organisation has worked really hard to train coaches on how to coach and produce athletes but virtually nothing or sadly little is available, as I write this, on how to develop the individual coach into a high performing individual and develop their strengths. This is such a book.

Introduction

You may already be a good teacher, leader or coach with considerable experience of working with hundreds of athletes or students for many years. You might know your subject inside out and can quote the greats of the game and reel off all sorts of statistics about top players in the sport. Or you may be just start- ing out, wondering how you can develop your love of the game into a viable coaching career.

Are You a High Performing Coach?

Increasingly, people are looking for quicker, quality 'how to' advice and learning programmes for less cost. Unless you can provide the solution that ticks all the boxes, your qualities, knowledge and experience very quickly fade into insignificance when pitted against the needs of to-day's discerning customer who wants results yesterday. Organising your coaching programmes in a way that helps your clients progress easily, learn the sport quickly and has them coming back for more all while telling others about you is what will make your coaching programmes successful.

By simply learning, applying and adopting a few of these strategies to your sports coaching philosophy and business, you will soon be on your way to becoming a high performing sports coach.

It is important that you commit to self-development and improving the level at which you operate and function as a high performing sports coach. Make a difference in your athletes' lives; serve them better and improve your quality of coaching by coaching in a style that makes you unforgettable. Be dynamic and memorable by making sure each training session is stimulating or challenging. Make effective use of your voice if you need to use it by varying your vocal volume, tone, and expression in order to maintain attention. You must be a coach people want to learn from and can relate to.

Introduction

High performance sports coaching demands that you bring your best to your field of expertise on a daily basis in order to challenge your athletes to reach a higher level. Your athletes will only believe in you and respond to what you are showing them if they can see and feel your energy, enthusiasm and presence. The key here is knowing who you are and to being authentic at all times. Do not be one person when you are training or coaching and a completely different person when you are away from it. Always remain 'in the zone' without losing sight of the bigger picture or target that you and your athletes have set. By remaining in the 'now' you will effectively eliminate outside influences which can act as distractions.

As coaches we train our athletes to focus: to concentrate their attention on one thing at a time. By applying the same focus on to what you are doing, saying and observing in yourself, you can improve your own coaching skills. You will be aware enough to correct the mistakes as they occur, in effect guiding your coaching to higher levels of performance.

As a responsible coach you do your utmost to bring out the best in the athletes you work with. You help them make changes that will allow them to adapt to the rapidly changing needs of the sport. When it comes to my own coaching, I know it is up to me to make the changes and be a high performing individual if I am to be of any help to anyone I coach. You cannot succeed without being a high achieving person first. Continually ask yourself, "What have I done lately to improve both professionally and personally?"

Why Does This Matter?

Personal performance is what sets us apart from the pack. Our strengths are the attributes we depend on to carry us through the most difficult coaching sessions. They allow us to be able to handle our more talented (and often challenging) athletes and sessions. They are the psychological assets that also enable us to identify what areas our athletes need to improve in order to make the most of their ability. If you want to become more effective at producing high performing players or athletes, who can deal with high intensity matches and life situations, if you wish to develop others successfully as individuals who demand excellence then it is time to take a good honest look at yourself, answer some tough questions in order to make the necessary positive changes.

This book explains the concept of 'coaching to excel' and presents a perspective gained from a number of sources. These include the thousands of hours of personal coaching experience; the study of Sports Performance Psychology and Neuro-Linguistic Programming; reading sports books and journals on human excellence; study of rehabilitation of sporting injuries and biomechanics, reading biographies and studying excellent performers; and from the lessons learned in discussions with high achievers as well as working with, and being trained by, some of the top sport, executive and life coaches in the country.

Sport coaching is a part of my life. It is not just a humdrum day after day repetition of the same old lessons and the same old drills. It is to me the ability to teach the same skill 320 different ways in one week. It is a series of fascinating challenges and exciting achievements. It is a springboard from failure into success, in spaces of time that can vary, from momentary to annually. An exhilarating trip of discovery of skills and abilities I never knew I had. And with it all comes the pleasure and thrills of discovery; a new way of teaching here, a big smile after a lesson learnt there, a tear of joy after winning and yet another 'aha' moment with facial expression to match. The kind of stuff you never imagine you could experience.

I have been a novice and I know what it was like. I also know what it is like to be where I am now. There is just no comparison. The learning never stops. Train your mind to always operate at an optimum so you can always think of new ways to improve your coaching ability. Find time to try out new coaching styles. Keep reading across other disciplines, so you too can move with the times and evolve. This will connect you with the world and what is going on currently and where the trends are heading. As a high achieving sports coach you need to be future oriented, constantly on the lookout for when an athlete reaches their targets and be ready with the skills necessary to help them on to the next performance level.

When you go into an unknown territory, you need a guide, someone familiar with the terrain, who knows where the pitfalls and the slippery ground are and can warn you. It is important to have someone you

Introduction

can trust to tell you where to put your feet. Someone who knows the tremendous reward that awaits you over what looks like an impossibly steep climb. Someone who can encourage you with their confidence. This book is one of your simple guides. Follow the advice and put the principles into practice with the peace of utter confidence. They work. I have lived with them all and I know you will make it.

Developing excellence and being a high performing coach is a process that demands high standards in not just your coaching but in all areas of your life. This book also provides quotes offering inspiration, a list of positive attributes to foster, specific examples of, and tactics for, implementing strategies for developing a 'coaching to excel' mentality on a day-to-day basis.

As a Tennis Performance and Mental Skills and Life Coach, I enjoy working with those who are determined and are prepared to do what it takes to be successful and to be champions in life. I draw heavily on my own early life as a young national team tennis and golf athlete as well as my own experience as a tennis coach. The lessons learned from the best coaches who have served as role models and from my lifelong programme of learning have been invaluable. You too can be a person that inspires others, by being a coach who excels. I hope some of these ideas go some way towards helping you to make a positive difference in the lives of those you coach and provide you with inspiration.

Chapter 1: What Does Being A Coach Mean?

According to the International Coach Federation, 'Coaching is an interactive process that helps individuals and organisations to develop more rapidly and produce more satisfying results. Coaches work with athletes in all areas including business, career, finances, health and relationships. As a result of coaching, athletes set better goals, take more action, make better decisions, and more fully use their natural strengths.'

Sports Coach UK gives the definition of a coach as 'the consistent guided development of participants to achieve their own personal goals.'

In a landmark comment, Sir John Whitmore, who authored Coaching for Performance describes coaching as, 'unlocking a person's potential to maximise their own performance. It is helping them to learn rather than teaching them.'

What Defines a Coach?

Ideally, a coach is someone who plays an instrumental role in shaping goals and providing adequate focus for success. A coach is a person who acts as a catalyst for unlocking hidden potential and maximising performance. Therefore, their role is to assist and motivate, rather than train, teach and educate. The relationship they share with their students is somewhat like a partnership. The mode of instruction is conversational rather than instructional or therapeutic, with a strict orientation towards results.

A coach is a person who assists people in identifying specific goals and achieving them faster, with competence and ease. They provide athletes with the required tools, structure and perspective to accomplish much more, through an accountable process. A coach helps in reframing beliefs and assists in creating a focal point for the athletes, helping them to reflect upon it.

Chapter 1: What Does Being A Coach Mean?

In essence, the coach:

- Brings a mix of tried and tested as well as new and innovative approaches and methodologies to help you to succeed.
- Creates a safe space to explore what you want and how to get there.
- Provides honest feedback about whether your goals are exciting enough to motivate you and whether you have a realistic and honest assessment of where you are now.
- Challenges you when you go off track and help you stay focused.
- Reminds you to celebrate your achievements.
- Offers proven alternative approaches on reaching your goal based on previous experiences.
- Draws from the experiences of many lessons: some more successful than others in order to develop a wide range of alternative success strategies
- Can help you develop more positive relationships with other coaches and athletes.
- Is genuinely interested in your success and will champion you.
- Will be a role model, demonstrating many of the characteristics needed to succeed.
- Will listen to you but may not always agree!

Essential Qualities of a Sports Coach

'I have always tried to be true to myself, to pick those battles I felt were important. My ultimate responsibility is to myself. I could never be anything else.'
— Arthur Ashe

As a sports coach you must be completely goal focused, aiming to help your athletes or students achieve their goals without much difficulty. Apart from emerging as a true role model, whom athletes can actually look up to; you also need to be a great listener and an eloquent speaker!

In addition, you are required to possess the necessary characteristics to be able to motivate and encourage others. With all these criteria to satisfy, a positive outlook is essential along with a constructive approach to problem solving and challenge management. Here are a variety of essential qualities every successful coach possess:

- An ability to succeed in actively involving yourself with other people and working with them for achieving common goals.
- Respect for how others work and think.
- An open mind with which to learn from others and support them in their learning process. Coaching, above all else is a mutually enriching experience.
- An ability to handle complex people as well as complex situations.
- A recognition of one's own strengths and weaknesses and a desire to work on personal development.
- An understanding of the value in empowering and helping others to remain motivated towards their goals.
- An ability to recognise the fact that coaching requires complete involvement of the person along with a free inter-sharing of skills and expertise. You see that your personality and the present state and form are just as important as your expertise, skills and knowledge base. For instance, as a sports coach, keeping fit is extremely important. You should be fit and agile to provide the right guidance in achieving your protégé's targets. In short, you must be able to convince students that you indeed practice what you preach.

How Can 'Coaching' Be Defined as a Role?

'The difference between ordinary and extraordinary is that little extra. Be all you can be. Dream big.'
— Dr. Ann Quinn

There is much more to 'coaching' than meets the eye. Sports' coaching is an art that requires you to analyse scientific data and grasp the relevant information before converting it into usable information that you can then apply to your coaching. This is perhaps one of the key reasons why

Chapter 1: What Does Being A Coach Mean?

sports coaching as a profession, differs from teaching, consultancy or training.

It covers more than one role to get the work done. For a teacher, the task is to teach a target group how to perform a certain task or a specific activity. He or she may choose several modes, including instruction and demonstration. A consultant aims at educating his target group on doing things differently or better, in order to enhance performance levels. As a trainer his task is to train his group in organising skills, focussing primarily on processes and systems.

However, sports' coaching has evolved into a distinctly different status. The overall aim is facilitating positive changes using different roles that are seamlessly molded into one. High performing sports coaches today are not only expected to be good at their skills but also to fulfil to some degree, a variety of positions: that of friend, mentor, leader, therapist, teacher, trainer, manager and consultant, all in one.

Although the athlete is considered to possess the required expertise to achieve the stated goals, the coach brings coaching skills as well as experience on related issues. The focus here is to ensure awareness and clarity, evaluating and recognising progress all the way, and improvising strategies to mobilise and manage change. These are changes that can either be focussed on responding and taking action or could be ones concerning changes in communication strategies, awareness or unique ways of relating to others. Therefore, 'coaching' has more of a holistic approach. It needs to impact the mindset of the learner in every way possible so that improvements can be achieved quickly with lasting results. It is also a very rewarding profession that thrives mostly on symbiotic equations where coach and athlete interact in a mutualistic way.

What Is It Like to Be a Sports Coach?

Many describe coaching to be a true calling, rather than a profession for making money. Come to think of it, the level of dedication required to inspire others to succeed can in no way be compared to a simple profit hunting profession. It is a task that is undertaken to fulfill one's passion, derived from an intrinsic desire to give back to an eager lot who seek attention and time. It is about spending hours and hours in mere conversation alone, aiming at perfecting skills and providing improved results.

Are You A High Performing Coach?

Coaching is also about sacrificing leisure and pleasure without hankering for recognition. It is about immensely exerting oneself in order to be able to deliver what is required. It is about striving to maintain yourself in such a way as to be of use to those who need you the most.

Sports coaches seldom seek recognition for themselves. Instead, they choose to derive satisfaction from the recognition received by those they are coaching. Most successful coaches choose to take up, and commit to, this exceedingly challenging profession because they love it and are selflessly dedicated towards helping others to achieve their goals.

Considering that coaching requires assaying a seemingly complex role, being a sports coach is no simple task. It's about being nearly perfect or at least worthy enough to lead by excellent example. It also requires immeasurable introspection and the courage to follow your heart when it comes to unleashing the wealth of hidden talents and qualities in others. It is about excelling in your own life and having a good understanding of what that entails while developing the ability to help others to excel as well! And that, for sure, is no mean feat since it comes with immense responsibility. You need to continually invest in yourself and strive for improvement as well as working in the best interests of each person you coach.

An essential aspect in a sports coach's life is this relentless reflection. You must keep looking into the mirror in order to convince yourself that you have been giving enough to those who need you the most. You need to continually resort to self-evaluation asking yourself if you deserve to be looked up to as a guide and mentor. Time and energy must be devoted towards examining the hearts of the people you are surrounded by. You must also determine whether you are spending enough time on your own development in order to improve and remain up to date.

I had just finished a coaching session and was busy packing away the coaching equipment when I saw a man striding purposefully towards me. My first thought was 'not again!'

The venue was located within a residential area and from the time I had started coaching there, I received complaints from some of the residents about the level of noise the children I was coaching were making with their laughter as they were enjoying themselves while learning and play-

Chapter 1: What Does Being A Coach Mean?

ing games. I had also been given restrictions on how to retrieve stray tennis balls (no stepping on the grass or through the shrubs).

The complaints had escalated from verbal to racist with hostile notes being left on my car windshield. So, you will understand why I thought that I was about to get another earful.

The man stood in front of me, pointed a finger, and asked, 'Are you the

Coach?'

I replied 'Yes,' and as politely and calmly as I could asked, 'May I help you?'

The next question took me totally by surprise as he said, 'Are you a good coach?'

'Yes,' I said, wondering what I had just let myself in for.

His immediate response was, 'Good, because I want you to coach my children starting tomorrow.'

I advised him that I would not commit to coaching the children if they were currently working with another coach and certainly not without meeting them first. My first responsibility is always to the players and what their targets are. As it turned out, I met the children, a brother and younger sister, for their first coaching session a couple of days later. Their love of the game was plain to see and their talent undeniable. I agreed to coach them both.

Within six months the father was out of work and the mother seriously ill. They could no longer afford to pay for my services. I continued to coach the players free of charge and soon, they were the top players in the county in their respective age groups. They remained there for the three years running that I worked with them.

Later the older child, who had gone on to study sports science, contacted me with a request to be his mentor while he pursued his qualification to be a fully licensed tennis coach. His dedication and hard work earned him a nomination as Tennis Coach of the Year. He is currently regarded as one of the top tennis coaches. His younger sister went on to be top tennis player in the college team and continues to enjoy playing to this day.

CHAPTER SUMMARY: So what does being a sports coach mean? In short it means that when the athletes come to you, you must be prepared in all ways to meet them where they are. Work to ensure you have the essential qualities of a high performance coach. You must continually strive to be the best role model you can be, all while wearing many different hats such as therapist, mentor, trainer and consultant. Maintain a positive outlook which enables you to encourage and elevate both your athlete's moods and emotions. And you do this because you have answered a calling to come alongside; out of a love for the sport and a selfless dedication towards helping others achieve their dreams.

 It has taken you your whole life to get to where you are now. Make sure the next step you take is heading where you wish to go.

Chapter 2: Excellent Coaches Build Outstanding Coaching Programmes

'Excellence is not a singular act but a habit. You are what you do repeatedly.'
— Shaquille O'Neil

If a teenage John McEnroe calls you 'Mister,' you have already earned a place in the Tennis Hall of Fame! That is exactly what Harry Hopman achieved. His place in history is far beyond coaching a young John McEnroe. He captained the Australian Davis Cup team from 1939 to 1967, winning it an unbeaten 16 times. His teams included names like Tony Roche, Frank Sedgman, Ken McGregor, John Newcombe, Roy Emerson and many others. Today the Hopman Cup is played annually in his honour, with this name featuring in the International Tennis Hall of Fame in Newport, Rhode Island and in the Australian Tennis Hall of Fame. Harry Hopman opened his own coaching institute, the Hopman Tennis Academy, in Florida, where he taught many now famous names in the game, including Andrea Jaeger.

While not everyone can walk in those particular shoes, you too can become a coach people look up to and seek guidance from. All it takes is passion and the right set of skills. The first step towards becoming an outstanding sports coach is to be your best and get the best training you can get.

Where Are You Now?

Before you can commit to going to the next level in your coaching career, you have to know where you are now. This is a very important stage which will require genuine honesty from you. Finding you have more work to do than you first thought might be a bit painful and can even be discouraging. You must be prepared to look at all areas of your life openly and truthfully.

Assess and take note of your weaknesses as well as your strengths. It is very tempting to focus solely on improving areas of weakness as we are prone to do when working with athletes. Make sure you acknowledge your strengths too. A word of caution: don't let yesterday's failures affect today's actions or condition tomorrow's hopes. Admitting shortcomings takes a lot of courage but does not mean condemning yourself. It simply means recognising the areas that need improvement and providing a focus and direction. It provides an awareness of your potential and excitement as you realise you have the resources you need at your disposal. You can reach your target in less time and have definitely more going for you than you first thought. You may also find that you have been conditioned by circumstances and people you associate with into accepting a certain opinion of yourself. Are you living up to your potential or trying to please those around you? Now take a good honest look and start making any necessary changes.

You are probably reading or listening to these words because you desire more out of your coaching life than you have had up to now and want to find out how to get it. In order to excel at what you do you must be prepared to make certain sacrifices knowing that truly worthwhile and permanent values will not just happen overnight. Decide to persevere despite the initial hardships because the long-term advantages are going to far outweigh the temporary sacrifices and discomfort. It takes willingness, commitment and determination, excitement and enthusiasm, as well as a good amount of fear and doubt as you make changes in certain ways of thinking which will affect your life and lifestyle.

To Be Outstanding You Must Be Prepared to Stand Out

To be an outstanding coach, you must have a deep urge to achieve and reach beyond that which is generally accepted. You want excellence. You must want to get to the very top by taking the first step in that direction.

> 'A journey of a thousand miles begins with the first step.'
> — Oriental Proverb

The simple wisdom of this old oriental proverb is a powerful key to success. The best course of action is action. I have found that keeping a clear mental image of my goal is a constant stimulation. Use visualisation and see yourself actually carrying out certain tasks. Picture the various ac-

Chapter 2: Excellent Coaches

tions necessary and watch yourself perform them. This mental rehearsal makes the actual physical act easier. It certainly stimulates you into action and it imbues both your conscious and subconscious mind with a clear and constant awareness of your goal and the steps or preparations required to achieve it. Setting goals and preparation takes effort. It requires planning, time spent in quiet contemplation and then practising and learning. When you watch professional coaches or athletes perform, they make it all look so easy, natural and effortless. But behind the style and prowess lie many months and most often years of training and preparation. Failure to achieve high goals is often just a lack of willingness to prepare.

There are three main steps in preparation:

1. **Skill Mastery:** Decide what training you need and start mastering the skills. Choose a training programme from a recognised coaching organisation and build a strong foundation for a successful career with the right credentials.

2. **Confidence Building:** The better you are at performing the skills, the more confident you will become. Sports coaching requires you to put in the hours of practical training. Be proactive in seeking out work opportunities. If this is not currently possible, take up an assistant's role and start learning from a more experienced coach.

3. **Perseverance:** Not everything goes according to plan every time. You need to commit and keep going regardless of the obstacles or opposition you encounter. Admitting defeat when the going gets tough makes it more challenging to start again. Discontinuing is a setback and momentum gained in your skill building process is lost.

Make a start until it is the right time to do what needs to be done next.

- If you are transitioning from another career into coaching, training is your best bet to succeed.
- If you want to work with large organisations and well respected teams, you need the right professional qualifications. Most institutions and agencies only hire coaches who are professionally qualified.

- Many organisations need their coaches to go through specific training depending on the membership, credential and accreditation of the body.
- The right training can give a competitive edge to your career.
- If you want your services listed on respected coaching directories, recognised training and membership to governing bodies is a prerequisite as they will often not list coaches without specific training.

Training does not stop at the initial accreditation phase. To remain competitive, it is recommended that all sports coaches remain actively coaching, take regular refresher classes and ensure continued education to hone their skills.

While sports might not change as rapidly as many other industries, modifications do come in with each successive generation of players. This makes it all the more necessary for coaches to be up to date with the latest techniques of training and strategising in their sport.

Good sports coaches are characterised by a strong sense of self identity that is reinforced into the psyche by experience and dedication. It is a winning identity that motivates, drives and inspires your athletes to excel. High achieving sports coaches are motivated by an inner commitment rather than a competitive approach that pits them against others. You must appreciate your importance in the lives of your athletes and undertake the responsibilities of being a trainer, motivator, leader, friend, guide, psychologist and mentor with pride. You appreciate challenges and consider obstacles as fresh opportunities to learn something new. Primarily, we humans are ego driven and sports coaches use this knowledge to bring about positive changes.

Coaches also have a strong sense of purpose. They are always prepared to acknowledge their expertise and scale newer heights of perfection. They are also inclined towards charitable work and are keen on contributing towards the greater good of the community.

Chapter 2: Excellent Coaches

Ongoing Training and Its Significance for Professionals

Mark Tennant has over 20 years' experience coaching in clubs and tennis centres in the UK, specialising in particular in coaching players aged 10 and under. He has been training coaches for the Lawn Tennis Association and International Tennis Federation (ITF) for 15 years, and has tutored over 90 qualification courses. More recently, Mark has been involved in the development and launch of the ITF Tennis…Play and Stay campaign and Adults' Tennis Xpress, working with the ITF and experts from other major nations. He also wrote the ITF Tennis…Play and Stay manual which has been translated into over 20 languages. Mark is a regular speaker at conferences worldwide and a member of the ITF Adults' Working Group and the ITF introduction to tennis taskforce, as well as training tutors for national associations. He is Coach Education Director of inspire2coach, his own company, which offers coach education worldwide and tennis facilities in the UK. Mark understands the importance of ongoing training and continually strives to create programmes that will inspire and educate.

Training programmes for sports coaches are offered by various recognised bodies and each programme targets a specific segment of the coaching professional's career. While some target beginners, others are meant for professionals at advanced stages of the learning curve. So, even if you are a professional coach in your own right, the need for ongoing training is unavoidable. In this ever-changing, fast-paced world of today, concepts are short-lived. What seems so very relevant today in a particular scenario, could lose complete significance within a couple of years. It is for this reason that, ongoing training and education is mandatory for knowledge that is up to date and relevant.

Learn as much as you can about your profession and improve your skills and performance. When you do not know what to do or how to go about doing something, the fear of failure is magnified. It is human nature to fear what we do not know. Fear of the unknown and fear of failure keep millions of people in jobs where they are unhappy and living discontent lives. Fear and worry saps strength, making you suspicious as well as pessimistic.

Ultimately it can stop you from taking action. Knowing your role, what it entails and what you want to achieve as a sports coach will spur you into achievement.

In addition, every sports coach should understand the kind of physical exercise required of him or her in order to maintain optimum levels of fitness. Nutritional elements are required as well. Even more importantly, is knowing how to coach in ways that will transform your athletes into purposeful individuals. With extensive research continuously being carried out in the sports industry, without ongoing training, you risk running programmes based on redundant modes and methods that are ineffective and possibly detrimental to young impressionable athletes. This could possibly lead to cost in time, resources and energy that any keen and dedicated athletes will not appreciate.

Undergoing periodic practical skills training, self-evaluation and study sessions are also vital for progressive skill enhancement. Coaching techniques have been transformed in leaps and bounds during recent years, given the large scale intervention of technology and the amount of money invested in professional sports. Training programmes, conferences, workshops and books are some of the best ways to be in the know about the latest in your field of expertise. Irrespective of the depth of knowledge and know-how a professional coach might possess, one who uses outdated techniques to impart training or to strategise is unlikely to see high success rates. Besides, reading and attending courses and training programmes also work in refresher courses that may be of use if a professional wishes to stay energised.

Choosing a Training Programme for Maximum Benefit

Depending on the stage of your professional career as a coach, the training programme you choose depends on a host of factors. Most of the choices you make regarding your training and studies should be specific to your personal growth and development needs. However, as a rule, always remember to choose a training programme or curriculum that has been offered by a professional body with all due accreditations and certifications in its favour. In order to serve your athletes better, look for reputable coaching bodies.

Chapter 2: Excellent Coaches

Search for answers to these useful questions before you make your final choice of training course:

- Are you looking for recognition nationally or internationally (or both)?
- Do you want to focus on skill development or is your focus more academic?
- Do you wish to specialise in a specific area or with specific athletes?
- Do you prefer a face-to-face training programme or would you like a more flexible programme, such as online or distance learning?
- Is the programme you are thinking of joining flexible enough to allow you to discover your own niche or to build on your strengths?
- How can you assure yourself about the quality of the training provided?
- What experience or qualifications do the trainers on the programme have?

How Does Training and Personal Development Create Outstanding Coaches?

'Don't measure yourself by what you have accomplished, but by what you should have accomplished with your ability.'
— John Wooden

While not everyone can be a Harry Hopman, we can all aim to be as good as we can get! An outstanding coach is no mere instructor or trainer. An outstanding coach is a person whom athletes look up to, as a guide and a friend. Consequently, you become a role model of sorts, expected to perfect not only your skill set but other aspects of your life that could have a bearing on your personality.

There are not many, if any, comprehensive training programmes that will help coaches achieve all of this. It is up to you to consider the gaps that need filling in your professional development in order to grow different strengths. Here are some reasons why it is important to focus on cultivating various skills to a high standard:

- A well trained sports coach will find that it becomes easier to attract athletes. Success always makes for happier people and more enthusiastic professionals.
- Most training programmes do not cater to perfecting soft skills, especially when it comes to sports coaching. Skills such as relationship management and handling people with difficult behaviours can, and should, be fine-tuned for generating maximum positive impact on athletes. Remain open-minded and look to learn from other organisations outside of your specific sport.
- Modern techniques for fitness improvement, both mental and physical, can be very useful. Professional sports coaches constantly look for opportunities to improve their fitness levels, in order to transform themselves into superior example setters. Healthier professionals with high fitness quotients are certainly more able to encourage aspiring players to challenge their limits and excel in their sport of choice.
- The better trained and more qualified you are, the easier it will be establish the value of your service to your paying customers.

It is worth mentioning at this point that you must learn from as many sources as you can. Determination and commitment are required! It is not all going to be easy but if you are willing to make the necessary preparation to plan each step and break down the obstacles, being suitably trained will help your professional standing. Learn from others. Keep your mind open to new suggestions and never think that you have got it all together and do not need advice. First thing you must realise is you need a mentor. To become an outstanding coach you need to draw from the expertise of others. You will need similar help, encouragement, advice that you dispense to your athletes. You must be willing to draw from those who have accomplished what you hope to become.

The secret is to absorb the principles of the knowledge and experience of others and then adapts them to your own way of coaching and to your character. Once you find a method, style or principle that works well, do not make the mistake of thinking you have found the perfect coaching formulae. There is always room for improvement and not every coach-

Chapter 2: Excellent Coaches

ing formula will work for every athlete. Read coaching reference books as learning will stimulate an appetite to learn more and you will be better able to apply what you have already learned. This is the same mechanism that is activated when your athletes learn and improve. They will be eager to not only learn more but want to try out the new skills at any opportunity they get. It also explains why your coaching session must always include a competitive element to encourage the application of your athletes' new found skills. Your aim is to transform into an outstanding person whose qualities your athletes will be eager to adopt.

How Training Programmes Equip Coaches

If anyone knows a thing or two about coach education it is Anne Pankhurst. Understanding the key concepts in talent identification and the development of junior tennis players are just some of Anne's specialties. Her dedication to coach education has seen her influenced sports coaching methods, trends and training programmes worldwide. Anne Pankhurst is currently the Education Consultant to the Professional Tennis Registry (PTR) with the responsibility for developing a new 3 strand, player-based coach education pathway at different levels for coaches in the United States of America and worldwide. She is the Player Development consultant for USA Football, working to construct six separate player age based coach qualifications. Anne also works with players and coaches in several tennis academies in the USA and the United Kingdom. She continues to lead by example with continuing personal education. She is a part time PhD research student at the University of Central Lancashire in the UK, researching the links in the development of potential for players and coaches. Previously Anne was Coach Education Director for the Lawn Tennis Association (LTA), before becoming Manager of Coaching Education for United States Tennis Association (USTA). In both positions she developed player development pathways, including USTA's progressive development of a high performance player. She is responsible for designing the Player Progressive Development Model (PPDM) for USA Football, as well as models for twelve other sports.

Here are some of the basic characteristics that outstanding coaching programmes tend to exhibit:

- **Mix up the top down and the bottom up approach:** Research has revealed that target groups certainly find it easier to learn when the mode of coaching is more participatory than instructional. Ideally, it should be a mix of the top down and bottom up approaches. Considering that the overall demeanour of the coach is an impactful one, participational coaching is likely to leave a high impact that leads to faster and lasting change.

- **Self-organisation and highly organised programmes:** Magnificent coaches, who are role models in their own right, remain highly organised and choose to offer programmes that are equally organised in form, content and sequence. With your personal attributes in perfect harmony, it becomes simpler for you to improvise the programmes when the need arises and with due clarity.

- **A healthy mix of ambition and humility:** Programmes created by coaches who are unusually ambitious often fail to connect to all members of the target group. Being overtly ambitious could in fact create a sense of disconnect among team members and the coach in charge of the team. Too much humility is not likely to work either! What is required is a generous portion of both traits. Goals need to be progressively ambitious, although they should be pursued with complete modesty. This is precisely why the coach needs a balanced personality, one that reflects both. It is imperative to be encouraging, not savagely competitive!

- **Engaged but detached:** It is very important for the coach to establish, perfect and employ interpersonal skill equations with team members. You are required to understand your athletes' interpersonal traits and come up with a programme that engages and motivates them to perform to their full capability. However, the programme must also provide a certain degree of detachment from you personally, so that you can remain focused on the common goals that the athlete or group has set out to achieve. Maintaining good rapport with members of the group is a good idea because more often than not, it is personal equations that pose hindrances in the achievement of goals.

Chapter 2: Excellent Coaches

- **Establishing work ethics:** It is important to encourage athletes from an early stage to grade their performances on the basis of effort, focus, reason, intensity, attitude and aptitude.

- **Consistency in teaching system and coaching style:** Players must know when and what to expect as they graduate to the next level of proficiency. There needs to be consistency in terms of the programme levels and in the coaching style so non-verbal and verbal cues, body language, personality and so on are not unpredictable.

- **Creating a positive learning environment:** Coaches need to ensure that their athletes have fun while they learn. You need to be confident yet positive, in order to put forth solutions that are believable. Attention must be paid to group dynamics when athletes are made to train together. It is imperative that you get to know your athletes and their personalities. Look to control or make use of the unique traits and tendencies in each athlete by amplifying, moderating or even eliminating them for the individual or group's benefit. Every athlete that comes to your coaching session should always be provided an environment that motivates them to not just be good but great.

- **Acknowledging potential, not just performance:** Coaching programmes that consistently raise the bar on individual or team performance help unlock real potential. Achievement needs to be acknowledged, while at the same time steepening the learning curve recognises potential by encouraging the acquisition or attainment of skill proficiency in less time. Challenging your athletes shows that you have high expectations and trust them to do well. They will hold you in higher regard and appreciate the opportunity you are giving them to show you – or show off to you and others – their ability or improved skills. If you fail to engage their natural competitive trait, they will become bored and disengaged. Competitive sport is also about winning and losing and the responsibility of winning and losing should be fostered in players on mutually agreeable terms.

- **Establishing trust and discipline:** Without trust, there will be no cooperation. It is important for teams of any number to develop trust for one another and remain disciplined. It is recommended that you improvise various ways for fostering trust and applying discipline. You need to be capable of bringing individual athletes closer to each other and also of introducing control and regulatory measures for a disciplined approach. Treating all players in the same way may not be the correct approach. Different levels of control could be necessary for different athletes and they need to be managed accordingly

- **Providing alternatives that are powerful yet simple:** As has been discussed earlier in this chapter, learning for sports coaches is an ongoing process. It is important for you to maintain a programme of study and regular training in order to unlearn older concepts and open your mind to newer thoughts and ideas. This will allow you to organise, appropriate and pass on these ideas to your athletes. In such cases, the programmes you devise need to position these new concepts powerfully, in line with your coaching philosophy, and be presented simply. This will make your coaching programmes more attractive.

Having a well thought out philosophy based on your core value principles will help clarify what you stand for and what those working with you can expect. You will be clear in what you are doing and where you are going. This will make you a better decision maker.

A coaching philosophy consists of the beliefs and principles that personally guide you. These fundamental values are at the base of every decision you make, whether on the court or in your personal life. You cannot fake your philosophy because it will shine through in your actions! As a coach, your philosophy will evolve throughout your career but will be based on those values you hold in high esteem and the ones you are comfortable sharing with and teaching to your athletes. Here are some key areas to focus on when forming the basis of your coaching philosophy:

- Decide what your personal coaching goals will be. What do you want to achieve as a coach?

- Decide what you want your athletes to take away from their time with you.

- What life lessons do you want to impart to your athletes? These may change each season and should revolve around deeper is-

Chapter 2: Excellent Coaches

sues than just the technical aspects of playing the game. An example would be the importance of good sportsmanship.

- Decide what constitutes success for your athletes. Achieving this level of success will include teaching skills as well as imparting your own personal values as to what success in life means.

- Once you develop a coaching philosophy, write it down. This will not only clarify it for you but will enable you to make it clear to your athletes and their parents from Day 1! By establishing this foundation, you are laying the groundwork for a dynamic winning strategy that will be hard to beat.

To put it simply, the coaching programme is a true reflection of the coach's personality. It derives equally from his own being, as much from his skill set and experience. The impact you create through your coaching programme and the way in which it is carried through depends a lot on how you deal with the rest of your life. You must have the skills to manage your occupation, health, wealth and mental states. The manner in which you manage yourself leaves a lasting impact on your athletes. Therefore it is vital that the principles you stress upon are reflected in your own being. This is precisely why great coaches need to be in top shape physically and psychologically themselves, besides being adequately experienced and educated.

CHAPTER SUMMARY: We have established the importance of making yourself the best possible coach through a variety of measures: ongoing training programmes and continuing education will help you develop professionally while working on your personal characteristics will ensure that you maintain high coaching standards. It is through developing these lifelong patterns that you will be able to build outstanding programmes.

 Book now to start or attend a training course, conference or workshop.

Chapter 3: Skills Every Coach Should Have

'Sportsmanship for me is when a guy walks off the court and you really can't tell whether he won or lost, when he carries himself with pride either way.'

— Jim Courier

Great communication skills are one of the biggest keys to making a difference in the lives of others. Being an outstanding coach demands that you not only are able to communicate effectively but that your personality, behaviour and attitude all match what you say and do at all times.

Outstanding Communication That Dramatically Impacts Learning to Improve Performance

Now you have done all the training and may have acquired all the necessary qualifications that allow you to work with developing athletes. All the planning and organisation that goes into your coaching programme will not amount to much, and have little if any impact on your athlete, if you are not able to impart that knowledge in ways that your athlete understands.

This will help further your professionalism as well as produce productive athletes, students and children that will be tomorrow's leaders and decision makers. The influence you have on your athletes should never be underestimated. You are in the business of developing athletes who are champions in sport and life by helping them realise as well as maximise their potential. It is your responsibility to ensure they understand the importance of doing their best when called upon to do so and stay the course no matter how challenging the situation in order to excel.

This is where you, with a positive and conversational demeanour, will be able to represent the sentiments of the team or individual during wins

Chapter 3: Skills Every Coach Should Have

or losses and create an environment conducive for picking up the pieces and getting back on track.

The world is looking for the coach who can speak, cast an influence and achieve positive results as well! You could be the one who can deliver what those looking for a results oriented coach are looking for. The results you could be achieving in your coaching programmes will position you as a high achieving coach. You can learn to communicate with every person that you coach in a way that they want to learn from you and remain in your coaching programme. Retaining player numbers in your programmes will help you generate a better income and enable you to serve more people and lead a more fulfilling lifestyle.

Keeping this perspective in view, the essential qualities that make for an excellent person for imparting knowledge and teaching valuable skills are discussed here. Improving your own skills will add value to your coaching and make a big difference to your athletes' lives. It will do the same for you in terms of your skills and your ability to communicate and your ability to earn more money.

So, what qualities does a trainer, educator, teacher or coach need to not only deal with an entire team but to handle individual egos in a way that takes each player or student to greater and greater heights? This is where a coach needs much more than sports coaching skills. They need life skills. They are a synthesis of psychosocial and interpersonal skills like decision making and value clarification. They are non-academic foundational skills humans learn and these have in recent years assumed significant importance to the role as coach.

Qualities Coaches Should Develop

Being a successful sports coach also makes you a catalyst for change and an instrument of success so you, indeed, have a significant role to play. Not only does your job involve perfect utilisation of your expertise but also complete application of your personal skills. Who you are, is just as important as how well qualified you are and how much experience you possess. Naturally, a complete array of skills are necessary to make a mark. Here we discuss some specific skills that form a good foundation for a successful coaching career. It is important for you as a sports coach to imbibe positivity. You will need the skills to influence not just one athlete but in some cases the entire team. Some of the most desirable qualities you need to possess include:

- The ability to bring out the best in your athletes.
- The courage to stand by your philosophy and principles.
- Not being easily influenced by styles. Styles must only be adopted when they are tried, tested and verified.
- The ability to foster respect for everyone and uphold professional standards.
- The ability to emphasise both temporary success and long-term performance.
- The ability to build a culture of continuous learning and impart knowledge in a way that is clear, concise and can be planned sequentially.
- To appreciate that developing athletes is essentially a team effort and every member of the team needs to be given due importance.
- To value the importance of remaining in shape physically and mentally yourself in order to set the right examples.
- To be organised and keep systems as simple as possible.
- To focus on learning new things and drawing inspiration from everyday solutions. The quest is to find better ways of doing things by drawing the best information, synthesising and creating something that is truly unique.
- To be constantly seeking new information and visiting different places in order to enrich and maintain a healthy way of life that promotes continued growth.
- To appreciate the fact that the drive for excellence comes from within. It is all about pursuing a standard in order to be the best.
- To love the job and possess a positive mental attitude coupled with enthusiasm and a healthy sense of humour. It is important for you to derive immense enjoyment from coaching and to remain motivated at all times.

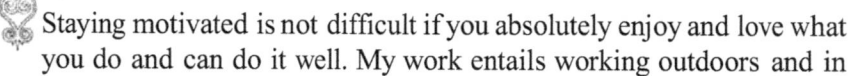 Staying motivated is not difficult if you absolutely enjoy and love what you do and can do it well. My work entails working outdoors and in

Chapter 3: Skills Every Coach Should Have

all kinds of weather conditions and having fun, just like being on holiday. My colleagues and friends, whose jobs confine them to the indoors while they work, often comment on how I never seem to get tired, am always cheerful and full of energy, even after 'work'! Coaching for me is a passion. There is nothing else I would rather be doing because I am lucky enough to have a job where I get to help people become better versions of them – young or old. I make change happen in their lives.

Even when I work without a team alongside me I know I am in the business of improving people's lifestyles. It took a long time for friends and family to accept that this was my 'job'. According to them, I was just playing and it was not 'real work' and so they did not quite encourage me. I did not help matters by declaring that I believed 'anyone' could do what I do. This I discovered was only part of the battle. You will often find that when you start to succeed, some of your so-called friends will not quite appreciate the situation you are highlighting in their lives. And that is simply that they are stuck and you are breaking out of the mold and circumstances they are entrapped in. I have found this to be true at many points in my life. It took me a long time to understand that I had, in a way, become a silent accusation and constant reminder of their satisfaction with mediocrity. This is something the competition naturally never appreciates. I have found though, despite the opposition of prejudice, emotional trauma, active opposition and sometimes hostility, my love for what I do and for my clients who expect me to show up and be at my best are motivation enough. I have worked in places and with people who fight change. I have had to accept solitude and being treated like a misfit. Challenging the status quo and out dated ways of doing things is mentally, emotionally and physically exhausting. Situations like this demand commitment, time, energy and single-mindedness. Thinking beyond any current difficulties you may be facing is not easy and there have been a few occasions when belief in what I do has been royally tested and I have chosen to walk away rather than risk my reputation. But all those times fade into insignificance when we push for the last time and come through victorious. The good this does for communities have far outweighed the reasons for staying the same.

Basic or Primary Skills for Sports Coaching Excellence

As in most professions, there is in sports coaching, a requirement for certain basic skills and prerequisites. One needs to be duly qualified with practical playing experience spanning across a few years in addition to having the practical skills and desire to lead others. It is the best all round coaches who are at an advantage. Societies, organisations and people in general are looking to engage an experienced coach who has a proven track record of managing teams or individual performance.

In order to excel, it is very important for sports coaches to model excellence so that they are able to demonstrate high integrity and the vision for what they wish to achieve. Naturally, to do this, requires a certain know-how and demands the acquisition and use of specific skills. You must accept that it is up to you and not settle for something that is short of perfect. Incompetence, meaning unacceptable levels of performance, should not be tolerated in yourself or those you are working with. Instead, you must hone the ability to break the task down into smaller steps and appropriate guidance needs to be provided as required, to the athlete for improving performance.

It is equally important for coaches to be consistent in their performance as well. A stable mentality, an ability to remain calm and resilient under pressure and not failing when pressure mounts are hall marks of great coaches. Apart from specialised skills, sports coaches have a responsibility to ensure that each athlete is also able to learn and take away essential life skills from each interaction they share as coach and athlete. To achieve this, coaches need to be effective, creative, adaptable, consistent and flexible. Most of all, they need to have exceptional communication skills.

The problem is, most coaches do not keep up with their own continuous professional development and hardly ever consider their personal development and performance. They have not taken the time to plan their professional career or put systems in place that ensure they stay on track in developing all areas of their lives. Most coaches get overwhelmed by the new developments in their profession and the work it takes to keep up with the new technology that is required for you as a coach to remain fresh, energised and on the cutting edge.

Chapter 3: Skills Every Coach Should Have

Another challenge for most coaches is that they were never trained or attended any communication courses to help them learn. With no guidance at hand it remains up to them to work their way through. By the time they realise things are not working out, they will have already lost athletes to other sports programmes and their retention rates will suffer. The coach is left with no choice but to go on a recruiting spree instead of athletes clambering to get on their sports programme.

What You Need To Do to Become the Ideal Sports Coach

> *'A good coach will make his players see what they can be rather than what they are.'*
> — Ara Parseghian

When you work towards becoming that 'ideal sports coach', there are certain skills that you need to build on, such as:

1. The ability to motivate.
2. The ability to make quality decisions.
3. The ability to communicate effectively. You need to be able to say what you mean and mean what you say, using easy to understand language at a level appropriate to the listener to eliminate unnecessary repetition and minimises misunderstanding.
4. The ability to provide personal reinforcement without creating a sense of contentment that may lead to arrogance. Athletes must feel good about their performance but must never lose the hunger to grow.
5. Recognise your strengths and be smart enough to seek help when you need it or delegate work.
6. Be observant towards every detail. Anticipate and expect questions. Assure the athlete when they do well and pull them up when focus or effort drops. You will be able to observe learning taking place if you pay attention.
7. Know that coaching is about the athlete and needs to essentially be athlete-led and so, in that sense, you should not perceive yourself to be the boss. You should possess the humility to give due credit to those who deserve it. It is immensely important for

you, the coach. to appreciate the problems of the athlete and be compassionate towards them.
8. It is equally important to adopt suitable styles commensurate to the needs of the athlete. Trying to force them to abide by the coach's personalised style of performance enhancement may not be the best thing to do.

Almost a year had gone by since I had attended one of the most enjoyable and challenging coaching courses I had been on. There was a lot technical information to assimilate as well as coaching techniques and practical demonstrations. We had to not only learn, but perform to a high standard ourselves to stand a chance of qualifying.

The tutor had stood in front of us and for a good 45 minutes had reeled off all this technical, tactical, mental and physical information on aspects of athletic performance without referring to his notes. The presentation was engaging and made it all sound easy. I decided there and then that I wanted to one day be able to do that and better.

Now here I was. A lot had happened in one year and most notably, I had gained another coaching qualification level, set up my fourth tennis academy and taken on five coaches. Here I was now standing in front of them delivering one of our weekly 30 minute 'review and plan' meetings. I stopped mid-sentence and savoured the moment as what I had just said sunk in. I had just achieved what my tutor had done a year earlier. Without knowing when and how it had happened, I had learned it all, fully integrated the strategy into my own coaching and was now helping my coaches do the same.

Well, going by the list of essential qualities an ideal coach needs to possess, there is a lot more to it than mere education, training and experience. In summary, these are some of the important steps that are necessary for you to take if you want to perfect your craft as a coach. The most important ones include:

1. Obtaining the desired educational qualifications, training and experience.
2. Adopting the complete set of directives for efficient self-management. For instance, one's health, career needs, money man-

Chapter 3: Skills Every Coach Should Have

agement requirements, and a whole assortment of critical and adaptive life skills need to be honed.
3. Learning how to develop relationships and manage them well.
4. Mastering the art of building an atmosphere that encourages learning.
5. Mastering complete goal orientation and crisis management.
6. Delivering high value service and high quality sessions

The Session

Preparation is the key to delivering a high quality and successful coaching session that promotes high engagement. Here are a few tips and techniques that you can utilise to make the most of your time and energy well spent for the athlete:

- Always approach a session fully prepared to ensure you are tuned in to your athletes and can focus entirely on them. This level of attention demands that you clear your mind of all thoughts, opinions, value judgments, prejudices and experiences. This amplifies your listening skills and ability to process information you are giving and receiving without interference and helps you respond to their needs.

- Review the session prior (if there has been one) to your current one. Make notes as reminders of what you need to accomplish in the next session. This may not go according to plan but it stops you trying to remember while in the middle of the coaching session.

- Do not condone distractions either of yourself or from the athletes during the session. Remove any potential sources of distractions like misbehaving or undisciplined spectators, handheld devices, mobile phones and computers.

- Pay extra attention to detail in all the fundamental performance factors and level of enjoyment being experienced by the athlete. Without which flawless execution cannot be attained.

Make sure your athlete learns something new in the sessions. They must always take away something positive from their interaction with you. This must be confirmed by them so do not make assumptions that all went well.

- Confirm the next session or steps or actions they need to take away from the session in order for them to achieve their targets.

It is not enough to simply take your athletes through the motions of training. Take time to delve deeper into learning and practising various aspects of your sport and become an expert. Books like Winning Tennis by Rob Antoun is a fine example of how to look for details in a players performance. Develop your knowledge base and the use of technology such as video analysis software which allows you to study, analyse and correct the finer details of technique or match play. To raise the standard of performance in your athletes requires an even higher level of engagement by you if you are going to spot minute technical flaws, tactical errors, physical inabilities, diminished focus or dip in motivation. Over and above all this, you need to learn how to remain focused and keep this check list in mind. Especially self-management, which is often neglected or taken for granted. If you value your career prospects and personal levels of performance, you will do what it takes to remain fit and enthusiastic and are more likely to become a living success like Larry Stefanki.

CHAPTER SUMMARY: The key with developing those tangible and intangible skills for coaching is to focus on those skills that make you a better person and athlete. Next pay attention to developing those attributes that allow you to come alongside and encourage another to achieve their very best. Becoming a high performing coach is similar to becoming a high performing athlete...take those innate qualities that already set you apart and continue to hone and polish them for a lifetime.

 Make someone smile today.

Chapter 4: Communication

'Keep it simple, when you get too complex you forget the obvious.'
—Al Maguire

Communicating with Your Athletes

More often than not, when we refer to communication, we inevitably think of 'talking'. One of the things a lot of coaches take for granted once they become comfortable with the athlete they are training, is the way in which they speak, their choice of words, manner and tone. Aim to use the 'right' motivational words that will make them play like the champion you are training them to become. Coming up with something deep and meaningful may not be required.

As a high performing coach, ensure you get to know the athlete. Although it is not always possible to say the right thing to them, you must get the partnership to a level where the occasional mistake can be easily dealt with. It is wrong to assume the athlete will be hanging on your every word all of the time.

The most important communication should be relayed well ahead of the tournament day. What effect your words have on the athlete depends on the trust and relationship you have built. It is about knowing who your athlete is as a person, how to relate and talk to him or her.

It is important to remember that athletes are just ordinary people.

Always Be Honest With Them

Although Larry Stefanki went on to win an ATP Singles and three doubles titles as a player, he will also be remembered as one of the greatest tennis coaches in the world. After all, when you have coached John McEnroe, Marcelo Rios, Yevgeny Kafelnikov, Tim Henman and Fernando Gonzalez and Andy Roddick, you must be doing it right. Under Stefanki's guidance, both Marcelo Rios and Yevgeny Kafelnikov achieved No.1 rankings, while Tim Henman achieved No. 4. Stefanki would always remind his players that it is up to the player what they think and not what the coach thinks that is going to help them perform at a high level.

How Do You Talk to Your Athlete to Get the Most Out of Them?

You will find, over the years, that reading is an excellent way to assimilate knowledge and wisdom without having to go through costly experiences to attain them. The biographies of successful people will give you many secrets on how to further your own success but you will still need to make time to learn, study and associate with others. It is time extremely well spent. The success process takes time, faith, patience and hard work. Recognising that you have failed in some way can be upsetting. This may have occurred because you were in too much of a hurry and missed crucial steps on the progression journey.

It is important to face the hardships and challenges as well as joys, savouring every victory and appreciating every small gain. Risk failure in order to rise from defeat and meet the challenge again without letting failure become a weight that holds you back.

When I started my coaching career, there were no courses or programmes that offered comprehensive training for all the areas I needed to develop. Unfortunately, this has not changed much over the years and a lot of the training being offered fails to meet the high standards that world class coaching demands. The training I attended did not show me how to communicate effectively with my athletes or customers and it has taken years of attending different training courses, seminars and conferences, at great expense, to find the right information. By using my failures as stepping stones I have learned to consciously overcome the discouragement that initial failure brings. This has taught me how to forego the natural inclination to feel sorry for myself and want others to commiserate with me and agree that life is not treating me fairly. I knew that the 'poor old me' attitude would drag me back into mediocrity and that thought was enough to snap me out of the negative attitude, shake myself out of discouragement and face the hurdle. I have faced many

Chapter 4: Communication

failures in my personal and professional life using this technique and not let fear of failure become a shapeless nightmare that haunts all my endeavours. I know that, sometimes, the thought of the effort and sacrifice of the work involved has deterred and delayed me from reaching towards a higher goal but not for very long. I enjoy success and keep trying to improve on what I know as I strive for excellence.

Coaching and knowing how to communicate success plays a major role in producing champions and mentally confident athletes

Developing and training young athletes is not all about the drills and exercises and games that coaches put them through during the coaching sessions. It is about making sure you understand how to communicate and coach each player as an individual.

Knowing that communication difficulties could occur between you and your athletes for any number of reasons, keep trying different ways. It is important that these reasons are not ignored. They must be considered and strategies developed to overcome them.

People come to you for coaching because they want to improve their ability and skills. By remaining approachable, open and friendly you will be able to develop good coach-athlete relationships and know each of the athletes you work with. Make sure you know how they learn, what learning modality they prefer and what type of coach they need you to be in order to help them achieve positive results. Depending on the nature of the player and their reasons for taking lessons, your coaching style will invariably involve or change between authoritarian, casual or co-operative.

Working With A Listening Athlete

Always look at how intelligent and motivated the athletes are and pay extra attention to the language you use to communicate with them. I personally never give up on a student until I know they have "got it!" It is absolutely vital to me that I get to know the players if I am to have their needs met

Are You A High Performing Coach?

Make a point of listening to all concerns from both the parents and the athletes and respond with appropriate feedback that reflects their needs. Keep all the feedback that you give positive and for the purpose of improvement. This must then be applied to training and coaching the athletes. It helps you know how to get the best out of them during each and every training session or match.

You have to understand what they need from you as their coach too.

As a coach, you work with different types of people. This includes all ages and ethnic backgrounds, those that are shy, not terribly talented or feel insecure about their abilities, confident ones, strong ones, weak ones and many more. Pressuring them and giving them expectations for performance to 'make' them succeed has not been known to work. To get the best out of each of the athletes you need to understand what motivates them to succeed because a 'one-size-fits-all' approach to coaching just does not work.

Below is a list of four types of athletes and the coaching styles you may use to coach them:

1. **Highly Motivated, Great Co-ordination and Skill (Delegation Style).** These types of athletes are usually good at sport in general. They may play more than one sport very well and are often picked for school teams and groups. They truly enjoy sport which appeals to their positive mental attitude, always keen to try different shots, learn new skills while challenging themselves. They tend to work hard at everything and do not require much interference.

2. **Low Motivation, High Natural Skill and Ability (Inspirational Style).** These athletes are very talented, but have lost their desire to succeed and tend to bore easily. It is up to you the coach to encourage, motivate and constantly challenge them. They often need a reason to perform at their best.

3. **High Motivation/Low Skill (Guidance).** These athletes love to work hard, but have very limited talent. Getting the best out of them and helping them become better is often the best way to approach their training. Patience and perseverance usually brings about positive results.

Chapter 4: Communication

4. **Low Motivation/Low Skill (Direction).** These athletes are less talented than everyone else and don't seem to have the desire to get any better. They tend to be disruptive and require a fair amount of attention within a group situation.

When Poor Communication Happens

'We learned about honesty and integrity...that you don't take shortcuts or play by your own set of rules...success doesn't count unless you earn it fair and square.'
—Michelle Obama

A lack of confidence can sometimes cause any type of athlete to act in an aggressive way if they are unsure about what they are doing or lack the necessary skills. You need to be sensitive and offer encouragement and support. To help an athlete with low confidence, use praise, support and encouragement to try and overcome the problem and help them regain or develop self-esteem

Not every athlete will have good communication skills to understand and respond to the interactions and verbal communication from you and others. High levels of patience are called for in these situations and once a minimum level of communicating is established, building on this becomes easier.

- Being a good coach does not exempt you from making errors some of the time. Assuming the athlete in front of you can hear you when they are hearing impaired for example is a common mistake that has caught many a good coach out. Do not be afraid of making mistakes. However, to persist in the mistake is, and is not acceptable.

- Athletes, especially the younger ones may not be mature enough to be able to put thoughts and ideas into words and articulate themselves clearly. Help with the right choice of words, discussing performance with them will help them start to build a good enough vocabulary to communicate with you.

- Be aware that your athletes are just as likely to have problems processing information and responding appropriately especially in situations where they feel anxious, stressed or under some form of pressure to perform.

Each of these types of athletes requires a different coaching strategy to get the best out of them. We need to communicate with each player in a way that works and gets them playing to excel both at the sport and in life.

Added to this, every person has a preferred learning modality. Your ability as a coach and the results you achieve with the athlete will mostly hinge on your ability to communicate, influence or get through to the athlete. Your communication skills will have to engage and establish rapport with every type of athlete in their own preferred learning modality. Verbal communication predominantly only engages the auditory modality. It is easier for the athlete to remember better what is being communicated to them if you engage all their senses. The human brain stores pictures, feelings, smells and tastes more effectively than words.

Being Able to Communicate Effectively

'In many ways, effective communication begins with mutual respect, communication that inspires, encourages, or instructs others to do their best.'

—Zig Ziglar

The importance of good communication skills cannot be over emphasised enough. Effective communication will help you better understand your athletes or situations and enable you to resolve problems, build trust and respect, and create high energy and positive environments where creative ideas and talent can flourish. Good communication minimises misunderstandings which can cause unnecessary conflict and frustration in personal and professional relationships. Use rapport to create a synergistic relationship with your athlete in order for you and your athlete to understand each other better. Using rapport to manipulate or influence the athlete's behaviour in a negative way will lead to mistrust and tarnish your credibility and reputation.

Communicating effectively will help you to motivate your athletes and start getting very positive results as a consequence.

Start by developing an understanding of how people filter information by deleting, distorting and generalising based on their experience

Chapter 4: Communication

of time, space, matter and energy. What the person believes and or remembers will affect how they understand the information. This affects how the athlete feels which, in turn, affects their physiology and behaviour. You must understand your athlete's preferred mode of thinking and learning, what engages their faculties, whether it is visual ('see' the world), auditory ('hear' the world), kinesthetic ('feel' the world) or auditory digital ('sense' the world). Knowing this will help you to understand how your words and behaviour or body language, no matter how subtle, can be read by the athlete and instantly affect their response. This helped me to appreciate how useful and easy it is for the athlete to learn a skill when they engage more than two or more senses. This increases focus by drawing all of their attention to what they are doing moment by moment.

Our brains remember better, things that are exaggerated or out of the ordinary. Use vibrant colours, pictures, sounds, feelings or make them funny. In conversation, always remember to listen to the predicates, descriptive words used, so that you can establish the athletes preferred representational system and their understanding. They will either be visual, auditory tonal, kinesthetic or auditory digital learners or a combination of two or more.

It is normal not to feel very confident in your communication skills when you first meet a person.

The main point here is for you to develop a variety of ways of communicating that make you easy to understand. Sometimes it helps to simply use simple and short words in short sentences that cannot be misunderstood. This can also be applied to physical or tactical demonstrations where the person can take in the whole and simple action to replicate. Identifying an athlete's preferred learning style is not an easy task. Some individuals are naturally quiet or reserved and may not say much even when prompted. There is no guarantee that the conclusion you arrive at after communicating with the athlete will be the right one as this may depend on how they are feeling, the situation, context and even possibly the location.

Pay particular attention to what you are being told. People are often coming to you to help them with a problem they believe they have. Common myths and beliefs abound in the world of sports and sometimes people will believe what they have been told or heard to be true. A classic example is how an incredibly large number of people refrain from participating or taking up particular sports in the misguided belief that they lack co-ordination. By letting you know this in advance, they are laying down an excuse in case things do not turn out as planned, or they are issuing you with a challenge to disprove that belief or indeed just 'fix' the problem. A few words of reassurance or carefully worded questions may soon establish that a number of other things like poor equipment, lack of time or poor eyesight could be reasons they had not considered and may be responsible for the poor initial performance.

Learning Styles - See, Hear, Feel and Think Like a Coach

Guard against making assertions about the usefulness of learning styles and their implications on the athlete's ability to learn or assimilate information in all its representational forms. Clear communication will help your athletes to focus on what you are teaching, to improve confidence and self-esteem or remember what they have learned. Other factors that support effective communication include your own personality matching your ability to make the lessons engaging, stimulating, interesting, fun, challenging and progressive. This leads to improvement and better performance.

The concept that a coach's role is to find out what the person is doing wrong and then set about fixing the problem is misleading. The coach should not only focus on correcting mistakes but on identifying and reinforcing what is being done right and how to keep doing the action correctly and better. Highlighting mistakes in an athlete's performance is not always necessary and only serves to make some of them feel incompetent.

The reason the athlete or student is attending the coaching session may also influence their learning in ways that may not be positive. Being made to attend by a parent or for lack of another sport option or convenience are often not positive reasons to sustain motivation. Individual attitudes, limiting thought patterns and behaviours may also affect their learning potential.

The reliability of different learning styles or the quantity and quality of the various components cannot be measured. This is not to say that the

Chapter 4: Communication

students will only learn if they can match their preferred learning style to the way you coach or teach, but using a variety of predicate phrases in the different modalities is going to make a real difference to how successful your communication will be and your outcomes. Learn to adapt your predicates to meet their preferred learning style. If you begin to use these you will increase your chances for creating rapport by communicating with them in a language they best understand. It will help the athlete to relax, a state known to be conducive to learning and thereby increasing the ability to produce desirable and outstanding results with your athletes. Take some time to experience the different learning styles and ascertain your own preferred learning modality. This will give you an insight into how you sound and seem to your athletes and possibly an appreciation for how they might feel when you are coaching them.

- **Visual learners:** They tend to use visual language which includes words and phrases like, 'I get the picture', 'show me how', 'it appears that', 'focus on', 'look how clear', 'I see', 'imagine' or similar words to communicate. They also memorise what they see so demonstrations are very useful to these athletes. They are good at using visualisation skills as well as having a keen awareness of the physical environment. Using colourful coaching aids and equipment like markers, charts and kits will help keep them engaged. They are very interested in appearances, shapes, sizes and, more importantly, often pay close attention to the body language of others. They often speak quickly with quickly grouped words and minimum amount of detail. The often unconscious information and subtle nuances in your facial expressions, stance or demeanour will quickly be picked up by them. It is advisable to keep verbal instructions to a minimum. Their strong visualisation skills enable them to simultaneously picture detailed and vivid movies in their minds and compare different options.

- **Auditory learners:** They are good at listening and pay attention to sounds and tone of voice. You will find that these athletes like to train to the sound of music and are quite happy to train in the gym where they can follow a planned list and order of exercise routines. They will respond well to verbal step by step instruction and words of encouragement although may be easily distracted by noise. Their speech is often modulated. Give them a chance to talk and share what they have learned. Using phrases and words like 'I hear where you are coming from', 'that sounds right', 'voice and opinion', 'listen', 'tell me about that', and 'let's have a discussion' will make sense to them. It is important that you position yourself in such a way that the athlete can not only see you but hear you clearly. Their keen auditory sense makes them capable of hearing insincerity in your voice. Make sure that the coaching sessions are organised and run in sequence as well as being progressive to keep this type of athlete motivated.

- **Kinesthetic learner:** This athlete learns best through feel and touch and likes to be rewarded with physical things they can take away. They actually have to do something in order to memorise it and like to have a go and experience what they are learning. Give them the opportunity to explore different ways of doing things like hitting, kicking or throwing a ball. They tend to be good at moving and using different types of equipment as long as they can get a feel for it. Their constant need to be active means they will need frequent breaks. Examples of typical predicates, phrases and words for a kinaesthetic or tactile learner include, 'it felt right', 'hang in there', 'hold on', 'handling this better', 'feels good', 'grasp the idea', 'hard to know' and 'start from scratch'.

- **Auditory Digital learner:** The auditory digital representation system enables us to organise and file information which we can call upon later to make sense of things around us. It is not dependent on any of our senses and can exhibit characteristics of all the other representational systems. An athlete with a preference for auditory digital may say, 'that makes sense'. They like, and are good at, figuring things out in their minds and will want you to present things to them in a logical manner but not necessarily make it easy for them. They like being challenged, are fast learners and make good tactical athletes. They are problem solvers and like to use computers. They have the ability to memorise by steps, procedures and sequences.

Now consider which of the above apply to you. It may help explain your coaching style and give some ideas of how you can develop other learning modalities to make you an even better communicator. This does not mean you will get on with every athlete you work with. It will, however,

Chapter 4: Communication

give you a better understanding of what to include as you deliver the coaching sessions.

There are two reoccurring traits in the majority of the most talented and higher performing athletes. They are always prepared to work hard but they like to enjoy themselves whilst doing what it takes to get to the top. This may sound like a contradiction, but the truth of the matter is those who are training to excel enjoy being challenged when they are training and preparing for competitions, targets or tournaments but they perform better when this is an enjoyable process. This will translate into serious fun. A great many high performance athletes are naturally intuitive people despite all the varying personalities and they instinctively know what is best for them. They appreciate, respect, and will listen to a coach who is always honest with them.

- **Learn to use your voice:** Create special moments by using words that touch the emotions or your team or athlete. What you say can be or turn into a defining moment or bring them to a point in their lives where they can change their ways simply by communicating positivity and letting them know how good they are.

- **Talk to the athlete with a clear, straight forward and gentle tone:** Use words that mean what you want to say. Being concise is important to get to the root of the problem quickly and get the message across without having to 'explain' what you are saying. Ask why the athlete is there with you.

- **Clarify understanding:** Ask the athlete what they mean, or understand, by what they have said. This not only allows the athlete to reinforce the information, it also increases their understanding when they are made to think it through and repeat it back to you in their own words. Not every athlete will understand the purpose of the exercise, drill or activity. Ensure they know what you are doing and why and the athlete understands what is expected of them.

- **Face the athlete:** Be honest, use clear words and phrases and always give direct answers.

- **Encourage your athlete to express or articulate their feelings by talking to them:** While some players are quite expressive in the way they talk and act, others are more introverted and do not find it easy to talk about their feelings. It often falls to you as the coach to provide the vocabulary that will enable the athlete to describe if necessary, what they are feeling and allow psychological issues like anxiety and fear to be identified and addressed. It also provides a way to receive feedback on what the athlete is experiencing during a performance so that technical, or indeed physical, factors can be addressed

- **Get the name right:** Use the athlete's preferred name. They will not like it if you keep forgetting their name or saying it wrong. It is a sign that you do not care. Do not assume they are happy for you to use the nickname you have heard their friends calling them either. It is little things like trust and respect that are the nuts and bolts that hold your relationship in the balance. They are the ones that come under the strain during times of high pressure and it is easy for them to become loose, compromising the structure and integrity of the whole relationship, if they go unchecked. Always make sure the relationship between you and the athlete remains intact. Choice of words is crucial in the preservation of the relationship.

- **Sport Etiquette:** Preserve the culture of the sport by talking to your athlete about its history. Make sure you tell them about the great athletes that have gone before. This is a great way to instill etiquette and a healthy respect and appreciation of the sport in which they are trying to excel. Take the opportunity to discuss their cultural background. Due to differences in cultures and expectations they may communicate in different ways. In some cultures eye contact is discouraged and exposing legs and head hair taboo in others. So you would need to find alternative verbal and non-verbal clues as well as show acceptance of their dress code. In so doing you will be communicating respect.

- **Take the opportunity:** Greet at the start and thank at the end, each athlete at every session. Ask about your athlete's motives when they act a certain way during a coaching session. Please note that it does not always need to be bad behaviour or action. Evaluating an athlete's motives regarding a particular area of their game or performance is an emotional issue that they are more than comfortable to discuss. There is no need to be heavy handed or use harsh words or tone of voice. They will usually

Chapter 4: Communication

have a very good reason for their actions and it is up to you as the coach to see it from their point of view. Appreciate that due to differences in values and ideas, your athletes may not always agree with the way you ask them to do something. They may also have their own way of dealing with situations in life. If you can understand this, you too will come to the conclusion that as coaches, we are responsible for their behaviour.

Be Transparent

Being honest with yourself and transparent in all your actions will build your athlete's trust and confidence in you. This authenticity requires a high level of self-awareness in order to control your thoughts, emotions and behaviour and, in most cases, for the benefit of your athlete. Seeing you expressing anger and disappointment in your athlete's performance will not help the athlete. Develop a deep understanding of your true self and accept your likes and dislikes. This could mean identifying where your strengths lie. For example, you may prefer working with juniors as opposed to adults. Acknowledging your preferences allows your true personality to come through without causing people to wonder and doubt your actions or words. Recognising this will help you decide what assignments you commit to in order to perform at your best. This will improve your self-esteem and reduce the stress that occurs as a result of inner conflict when you do something because you feel you have to, as opposed to wanting to.

Coaching to excel is a high risk, high return pathway. Most coaches coach everybody and anybody (more club coaches than performance coaches) and have very likely been in your shoes quite a few times. A coach that is not clear and has not communicated the training plan will cause an athlete to stay up all night long, wondering to himself: what is this coach doing with my money? Are they making the right decisions and am I on track with my targets? Are they telling me the truth? And more importantly... how can I be sure and tell if they are not being honest?

Communicate Progress

Dr. Ann Quinn has helped a lot of her clients achieve their greatest dreams from winning Wimbledon and becoming world champions to winning gold medals, as well as coaching high achievers from all walks of life to excel in their chosen field and win in the game of life. By creating a winning game plan you can achieve your highest potential. Ann has helped many athletes achieve their greatest successes, from winning Grand Slams to guiding executives and performing artists to achieve their dreams and create the life they love. She is also a professional speaker and has inspired audiences in more than 20 countries and over six continents. She has written numerous articles, and authored and co-authored several books. Ann sits on international committees advising on professional development and sports science for elite athletes and has travelled the world extensively helping her clients to win.

Progress… it's the Holy Grail that separates you from being a measly coach versus being a coach in pursuit of excellence. A high performing coach executes, with or without money. You might not get as far or fast without money, or you may first have to make a choice between risking other areas of your programme versus eliminating player development risk, but at least you're moving forward. Often once you are moving, the laws of physics kick in and you will gain momentum. Athletes (and their parents or sponsors) want to hear about, and see, progress.

This can be shown to your athlete through quantified and measurable data like match analysis, video analysis, precise and timely positive feedback and so on. In so doing, you will be anchoring words and images of progress, improvement and even high performance or excellence in the athlete's mind.

An alternative would be to set up the training programme in such a way that failure to progress or improve is not an option. Coaching to achieve excellence means, making every coaching or training session real. Like life, there are no second chances. Life is not a rehearsal so going through the motions is not an option. If you are training for match play at whatever level, ensure your athletes understand what is required of them and the situation they are preparing for. Everything has to be done to the

Chapter 4: Communication

highest intensity, level of commitment and effort. Coaching to excel will produce players that excel, so no situation is left to chance.

As a high performing coach, your choice of words is very important in getting the right message across. Working with talented children or older athletes and adults, I have often found they can be very sensitive to the smallest of things. From voice tonality to perceived eye shift. The key is to choose the right words to communicate how much progress the athlete is making. For example, instead of saying: 'You are making less mistakes,' you could say, 'Your accuracy is improving.'

CHAPTER SUMMARY: Developing and understanding these communication skills and learning about what suits your athletes will enable you to build rapport much more easily and quickly. Using the right predicates and or mirroring them are further ways of establishing the relationship. From dealing with parents and sponsors, to molding the minds of the athletes in your charge; excellent communication will set you apart. Good communication is the foundation of any successful relationship, be it personal or professional.

    Pause before responding so you can hear yourself speak.

Chapter 5 : Stop, Look And Listen

'Perception Of Reality, Remember it is not what you say or how you say it, but rather what is heard that is important'
—Ian Gray

Ask Them About Themselves

You must be interested in a wide view of your athlete's life; what they do away from training sessions, where they have been, and what their personality or lifestyle choices. The more you are aware of the whole person, the more you can gauge what an impact you can have on their life and game.

Avoid complications and misunderstandings down the line by sharing your philosophy and ground rules up front. This should help communicate to them that you are there to help find a solution to their problems and let them know what you expect. You will only work with people who want to work with you. Any athlete, who is not comfortable with the rules or your way of working, has the choice of whether or not to commit.

Do not be afraid to ask deep questions:

- Why is the athlete there with you?
- What would they like to accomplish today?
- Can they tell you more about their problem?
- What level have they reached in their training? This is great way to confirm where the athlete believes their skills are.
- What happens if we don't find a solution? Will they give up, try another coach, try another sport?
- Express concern when they are not paying attention. Find out what is stopping them from giving you their full attention.

Chapter 5 : Stop, Look And Listen

- Let's talk cost (economics), what are they willing to invest in getting a problem fixed? Let's talk about dedication to training and practice in between lessons and putting what they learn to good use.
- What is the cost to them if they do not get coaching from you?
- What do you mean by that? – Specifically the words they have chosen to use.
- 'Let's do this' – allows you to set a process or at the least creates a platform from which to initiate one
- Who else is involved in this training and will be interested in the athlete's progress? Is it the parents, other coaches, trainers or friends?

High Performance Seeing

> *'You knew my father?' — 'Correction! I know your father'*
> —Simba/Rafiki, The Lion King

As human beings we often take our senses for granted until there is a threat of losing one or more of them. We often look at things but do not take time to see. Developing the habit of paying attention to what you are looking at is a skill top coaches hone through experience and hours upon hours of observation of different athletes or skills in action.

Learning to use your eyes appropriately to communicate is probably the most powerful non-verbal aspect of communication and yet the least trained in the context of coaching.

Learning to stand back and observe the athlete perform will allow you to be more objective when it comes to understanding how best to help the athlete.

- It physically distances you from the action and gives you room to read even more subtle forms of body language such as the tensing of the jaw line and to calibrate an athlete's state.
- It allows you to become emotionally detached so that the feedback is concise, relevant and specific.

- It gives you room and time to think about what you are seeing, work through the options and reach a calculated and more informed decision before interrupting or giving feedback.
- It communicates trust to the athlete if you show that you can stand back and leave them to get on with it. The athlete is more relaxed and this frees them up to actually perform at their best as opposed to having you breathing down their neck, so to speak.

Eye Contact

Make eye contact whenever you talk to someone. It is very difficult to not stick to the truth when they or you can look into the eyes.

- You will be able to tell if they are paying attention or their mind and thoughts are elsewhere.
- You can tell when an athlete is in distress, i.e. playing through an injury, as the discomfort or pain will be reflected in their eyes or facial expression.
- Understanding some of the more universal signs such as rolling of the eyes, eyebrow raising, wide-eyed shock and surprise are all part of the communication process worth understanding.
- On occasion, you may be able to tell when an athlete is feeling unwell and failing to focus due to dizziness brought on by exhaustion, hunger, heat illness and possibly a more serious medical condition.

There is always more to your athlete than meets the eye.

High Performance Listening

Listening in order to help someone is a skill every high performing coach should be good at and requires ongoing practice. This is because it is a mental skill that demands more than your hearing ability. You must first take in what the other person is saying then extract the meaning from that information before making your own value judgments and coming up with an appropriate response. In this case, coaching for excellence demands that you engage more than your sense of hearing. High performing coaches listen and read emotions while deciphering the visual

Chapter 5 : Stop, Look And Listen

information being taken in by the eyes. This is why it is important to look at the athlete when you are speaking to them, not just because it is the polite thing to do. Choosing to associate or dissociate your 'self' from the feelings or tensions of the conversation may affect how you respond.

Qualities That Will Help You Be Better At Listening:

- Respect your athletes – just because you are the coach does not take away the fact athletes are individuals who have every right to be heard and, yes, listened to. Be patient, show consideration for the position your athlete is in. I am always pleased when athletes have the confidence to talk to me because I know that it will be easier for me to use that open channel of communication.

- Pay attention to what is not being said. You need to listen to the words that are being used and hear the person's intent, otherwise misunderstandings will occur.

- Look under the surface. When an athlete says 'I can't play with this ball', it will not help the situation if you challenge that statement directly. Instead, use a more probing question to get to the real issue. What is it about the ball that makes playing impossible? What solutions does he have to resolve the playing or the ball problem? Ask when the athlete lost their ability to play or when the ball became useless? What changes have occurred in the ball or in themselves to render the ball unplayable? More often than not, you may find that the statement has nothing to do with the athlete's ability to play or the quality of the ball

- Decipher the truth. Listen to what is being said and how it is being said. Do not rush to answer before you have heard what the athlete is saying. It is tempting to start constructing the response before the other person finishes speaking. You will miss valuable information as your mind will not be able to understand the whole message or their point of view completely.

- Repeat what your athlete says to check for understanding and meaning. I sometimes find in question and answer sessions with a team, it helps if others hear the question and focus on the discussion in hand. Quite often members of the team will answer saving me from responding. I view these moments as absolutely valuable for the learning process for many reasons. It allows the athletes to learn from each other (also known in the executive world as peer coaching), a very powerful and effective tool. It enables quick assimilation of information as they understand the athlete's use of a language, style and syntax. The coach is able to observe the interaction from a dissociated position which requires little, if any intervention.

- Pay attention to your own body language. As a coach it is important to maintain a positive mental attitude and open body language while remaining present with your athletes. Most people simply listen to the words that are being said to them, but words contain only 10% of the message. The remaining 90% is hidden in the body language and the tone of voice.

Active Listening for Coaching

Even with the best of intentions, messages can become distorted and confused. Sports coaches who learn to listen well and provide effective feedback will improve overall dialogue reception.

You are listening actively when you:

- Pay attention and be sincere in your desire to hear the other person (instead of mentally practicing what you are going to say next).
- Commit to using any conversation as an opportunity for you to learn from the other person.
- Relate to his or her perspective, seek to understand and empathise with their point of view.
- Reflect on what is being said, synthesise the information, emotion, and feelings in order to improve understanding.
- Clarify by asking probing questions and validate perceptions and assumptions.
- Remain fully present and focused on the other person as they speak.

Effective communication allows a shared understanding between you and athlete which fosters a more positive relationship. Your athletes expect, and want, you to be dynamic, enthusiastic, knowledgeable and well

Chapter 5 : Stop, Look And Listen

informed. They look to you for credibility and expertise. They need to be confident that when they ask you a question, you will answer them effectively.

> **Be Unique**—To become a high achieving sports coach you will need to draw from the expertise of others. You need help and encouragement. You need advice and you must be willing to draw from every available source. This does not mean you must apishly copy everyone who seems to have achieved anything. The secret is to absorb the principles of their knowledge and experience then adapts them to your own way and according to your character. To slavishly imitate someone is to be a poor carbon copy. Never an original.
>
> **Pursue Excellence**—Assimilate knowledge and wisdom and start being extraordinary. Become an expert in your field and set high standards for yourself. Being good in today's economy is no longer good enough if you are to maintain positive cash flow. Make sure you are selling yourself in a way that people will listen to and serving with distinction.
>
> **Service**—Customise your service and treat each person as an individual. Always give more than you are paid for. People want to feel valued and there is no harm in giving individual advice specific to an athlete within the team. Differentiation will ensure that each member is challenged based on own ability and is not held back or pressurised to keep up. Sometimes a word of encouragement is all it may take to raise an athlete's performance when they lack self-belief.
>
> **Caring**—It matters. You are there for the athlete. Make sure they get the most they can out of each coaching session. They are supposed to be learning and growing with every interaction they have with you and your responsibility to ensure they do.
>
> **Enjoy**—Learn to inject humour and storytelling in to your coaching sessions. It provides a perfect opportunity to use metaphors, a very powerful yet fun way of making lessons unforgettable. This will decrease stress and tension, cultivate a relaxed atmosphere and show your athletes that while your training ses-

sions may be focused, hard work and serious, you too like to have fun and enjoy working with them.

I remember a time when I was coaching a group of 7 to 9 year olds in an after-school session and I used a saying that the kids found so funny it stopped play for a good 10 minutes. One kid was laughing so much he wet his pants – which sent him and the rest of the group into fresh fits of laughter. Everyone in school heard about it and for months after that, a mother would call out to me 'No Jokes!' before each coaching session. None of the parents believed me when I said that I had actually been serious and not telling jokes at all. Still, the kids have never forgotten that lesson and what they learned. None of them can remember the exact words I used and I refuse to tell them!

Laughter reduces the level of stress hormones like cortisol, epinephrine (adrenaline) and dopamine and increases the level of health-enhancing hormones like endorphins. Laughter increases the number of antibody-producing cells for a stronger immune system. The key is striking the right balance and type of humour you choose. There are many ways of having fun and a good laugh without resorting to jokes involving race, creed, religion, gender and ability.

One of my operating philosophies is to never say 'no' to someone who wants to learn. However, I have on occasion said 'no'. It was in response to a request to coach two high performance players and, in both cases, they believed I would jump at the chance to coach them just because they were really good players. In fact, the reason I turned one away after our very first session was because he had the unfortunate habit of using bad language regardless of who he was talking to. The other I had found out beforehand was a smoker.

I chose not to work with both of these players and to help them eliminate their bad habits because this was not the reason they sought my services at the time and I had other athletes in the training programme to consider. These are not habits or behaviours I would have condoned in these athletes had I been working with them at an earlier stage.

I always let my athletes know how much I appreciate the opportunity to work with them. I let them know that I am there to support them in their training development and how much I want for them to succeed.

Chapter 5 : Stop, Look And Listen

This is just one way of communicating to them what I stand for, what is important to me and how I do not want to let them down. The most important message I can get through to them is that of high expectation. A lot of the best athletes I have worked with are very strong-willed. They are very confident in their abilities. The player may not always be on top form so it is up to me as the coach to remind them when the going gets tough and believe in them no matter what. If I have any doubt about their ability, it will show and the athletes will pick up on it. It is very important to show that I care and believe in the athlete's ability to do and be the best they can.

For this reason, athletes often take on more responsibility for their training in the knowledge that they have high standards to fulfill in order to live up to your expectations. Producing high achieving athletes will attract like-minded people to your training programme.

It is acknowledged that sports coaching can be challenging and stressful and requires a coach to call on their mental reservoirs to sustain and remain focussed. A sports coach should never take any conflict with athletes personally and any disagreements should be handled professionally. Athletes need to trust you, so a supportive and caring personality will be of benefit as well. Communication with the athlete at this level affects how they perform and motivates their positive mental attitude and confidence. By all means, make effective use of communication technologies like email or other forms of social media to improve efficiency but do not forget the usefulness of 'traditional' face-to-face interaction.

Having a pleasing personality will make you approachable. How you present yourself and ease of access to what you have to offer is also important. Athletes and their parents are so used to being approached, invited to training programmes and are bombarded with offers to be coached and to play for various teams. The good news is the majority who seek you out will actually be looking for what you have to offer.

As well as having a passion for your sport, you need to know your audience and enjoy working with them. Athletes appreciate coaches who are organised and show a seriousness of purpose and professionalism. If you want to make changes that stick you must have credibility. Never lie, orally assault, physically assault, ridicule, or attack based on race, creed or colour. Great coaches have practiced political correctness all their lives, not because it is was ever politically correct, but because it's simply the right thing to do!

When you meet a client for the first time, in the course of establishing the basic information, you will find out where they are from. Note when they are from a country that is different from yours and make an effort to learn about their culture.

An experience I once had that helped me learn to do this as part of my coaching came very early on in my career while working at an international school in Africa. This is a school that is responsible for expatriates children's education. After a few lessons, I noticed that the student I was working with could do just about every skill I asked of her very well. She could throw the ball to various depths/lengths and heights, at different speeds and direction as well as catch with unerring accuracy. When it came to using her racket to hit the ball, her swing, racket handling and timing of the ball was also really good. The player was really pleased with the progress she was making, as was I. None of this was an issue and she could do all this and more using her left hand even though she insisted she was right-handed. I then suggested she use her left hand and work as a left-handed player. Her response surprised me. She confessed that she was in fact left-handed but in her culture it is frowned upon to be left-handed and so she had to learn to be right-handed. She explained that in China, where she is from, she was not allowed to use her left hand to write. I read up on this and asked a Chinese friend, who happens to be a teacher and found this to be true. So now I make a point of finding out whether reasons are medical, cultural or personal.

It Is Not Just What You Say

Other forms of communication are conveyed through body language, behaviour and how you present yourself to the world. The way you dress should reflect who you are and what you stand for. Great coaches are often held in high esteem and are trusted pillars within their local environments and are seen as role models whether they are at work or at home. It is important for you to build a reputed brand of yourself over a period of time and realise that high service and product quality are building blocks of a good reputation. As a consequence, relentless hard work and patience is required at all times. Remember that you re-

Chapter 5 : Stop, Look And Listen

main an ambassador, not just for the sport you represent, but the sports coaching profession as a whole. Sports coaches need to operate with the highest integrity, sincerity, energy and enthusiasm, while being inspirational and having strategies in place for making a long-term impact.

Building and Cultivating Relationships

> *'When as a coach you find what works, share it, so other coaches may learn and develop.'*
>
> —Rob Antoun

Rob Antoun is a former Association of Tennis Professionals world-ranked tennis player who has coached at an international level over a 20-year period, including two British senior No. 1 ranked players and a Top-20 world-ranked junior player. Rob is a Performance Coach and is a Tennis Europe and Lawn Tennis Association (LTA) coach education tutor. He holds a degree in Psychology and has written two books on playing tennis, Women's Tennis Tactics published by Human Kinetics and 101 Drills for Youth Tennis. He also served as a national coach for the LTA from 1994 to 2002.

Coaching is essentially about personal engagement and it is essential for you to master the art of building and nurturing relationships. You need to be a good listener and equally good communicator in order to address problems comprehensively and provide plausible solutions. Your ability to deal with diverse personalities within your team or working environment is important and hence, conflict management has become an essential skill to master. This should be complimented by having or developing the skill of managing difficult people so that your energies can be channelled positively. Relationships have the ability to act as bridges that help in the mutual sharing of values and qualities. They need to be nurtured and built over time and with special care.

Often, the equation shared between you and your athletes emerges as the true essence of success. Being considerate, humble, expressing humility, compassion and empathy have a major role to play. Empathising, however, in no way means that you should be lenient about hard work and achievements. Being empathetic towards others' shortcomings will only help in recognising their limitations and finding ways of tackling them. This is what also creates an environment of acceptance that eventually leads to positive learning. There is no friction, denial or sharing of negative energies.

Apart from the relationship you have with your athletes, there are several other relationships that you need to succeed in your endeavours. For instance, you should be able to build healthy associations with your peers as well as your role models. A healthy relationship will fuel easy exchange of thoughts and beliefs that will help you as a coaching professional to rectify your mistakes and upgrade your skills.

The Circle Of Influence

Parents, physiotherapist, trainers, friends, teachers, girlfriends and boyfriends are all part of the athletes circle of influence and are worth consulting at the earliest opportunity. Everyone needs to be pulling in the same direction for the benefit of the athlete and the responsibility of ensuring this may fall to you. It may be necessary to re-educate the parents and friends who may not have a good understanding of what the athlete needs or the role they play at different stages of the athlete's development. Find out from the athlete which parent you get to report to. Establish their involvement and no matter how uninterested they may be, keep them informed of the progress and how the programme is going. Make full use of the opportunity when you meet them to:

- Thank and show respect and professionalism for the valuable responsibility to work with their child
- Confirm how they prefer to be kept informed (some parents want a blow by blow account after each lesson)
- Establish who the key people are on the team are and level of involvement with you and the athlete
- Convey belief in what you do and your capability to help their child

You may have to call upon your leadership skills in order to manage the team. Do not forget to include yourself in this equation as you:

- Connect and align the team members whose co-operation may be needed to create a team that understands the vision and strategies to support the athlete's development

Chapter 5 : Stop, Look And Listen

- Share the vision of what you and the athlete believe is possible and establish a direction
- Create the training programme and allocate the resources in time, equipment and energy necessary to achieve the target goals

Generating Learning

As has been discussed earlier, unlike teaching or training, coaching is all about inculcating learning habits and encouraging those you are working with to master new skills. Eventually, even this becomes a habit and a natural response to new information, skills or actions that you face on a daily basis. Perseverance and commitment will help you develop this attitude in yourself and your athletes. It will become yet another conditioned pattern of training in the same way that any habit is formed by simply repeating any action often enough. Any relevant and specific skills meant for generating the learning habit are mandatory.

You need to utilise the positives in your personality, along with your specific soft skills, to inculcate the best learning environment. Curiosity, asking questions and interactive learning needs to be encouraged. It has to be more of a give and take of ideas, with plenty of practical intervention. Instructional teaching alone might not be enough to develop a positive learning environment that promotes questions and encourages out-of-the-box thinking and unconventional learning.

Goal Orientation

Goal orientation is an essential quality for a coach. The tasks must essentially be aligned to the goals set in agreement or accordance with what needs to be achieved. As a coach you need to have the foresight to set appropriate goals, based on realistic parameters. They should be progressively higher and have plenty of action planning directed towards achieving the goals. Keep track of the time it takes you to achieve goals before establishing new ones. You will attain each goal step by planned step, one goal at a time and you will find that the time between goals will probably become shorter and the goals themselves higher. These records of success, no matter how small, will keep you motivated and able to maintain the momentum of success.

Are You A High Performing Coach?

You will also need to exert your influence and power to keep the entire team in sync with the goals and have contingency action plans ready for those who fail to fall in line. The team in this case may include parents, organisers and administrators who may turn out to be firm supporters of the sports programme or frustrating distractions that jeopardise your efforts. Each hurdle that comes in the way, including changing behaviours of team members, crumbling under pressure, loss of motivation etc., need to be managed with dexterity, so that the team members do not lose sight of their collective goals.

CHAPTER SUMMARY: It is vitally important that you take an interest in your athlete's life outside of simply coaching their athletic skills. This person (or people, in the case of a team) depend on your ability to think one or more steps ahead whether within the session or long term. They expect you to know what they need before they do. You do this by:

- Actively listening
- Paying full attention to detail
- Asking questions and listening to the answers!
- Getting involved in your athlete's lives
- Staying tuned in to what you hear and paying attention to what you say

Work on those areas that you need practice on, in order to be a great listener. Stay tuned into what you hear so that you can effectively coach.

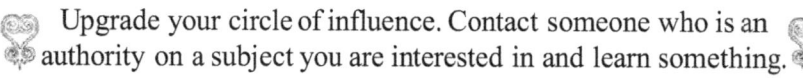 Upgrade your circle of influence. Contact someone who is an authority on a subject you are interested in and learn something.

Chapter 6: Long Term Self Development

'What the society thinks is of no interest to me. All that's important is how I see myself. I know who I am. I know the value of my work.'
—Robin S. Sharma

Tony Roche is probably one of the most successful coaches in tennis history. He has worked with some of the most accomplished tennis players, including four top seeded players, Ivan Lendl, Patrick Rafter, Roger Federer and Lleyton Hewitt. Roche also coaches junior players for the ATP junior pro tours. One wonders how Roche still manages to pull success stories. The secret is self-management.

To begin with, you need to be able to portray immense self-confidence by appreciating and understanding that you are indeed an instrument of change. You need to work on your emotional intelligence and practice controlled assertiveness in order to push your athletes or team members hard enough to challenge their limits. Your self-management skills should also comprise personal maintenance and upgrades, so as to remain in top form. You will need to impose measures, including the right diet, to maintain good health and preserve fitness levels and agility. As a healthy coach you are more likely to be respected and looked up to. It remains every coach's responsibility to engage measures to improve their self-confidence, reduce daily stress and strike the right work-life balance. This is done so that one can remain enthused, happy and productive.

In order to excel, it is very important for sports coaches to model excellence so that you are able to demonstrate high integrity and the vision for what they wish to achieve. Naturally, to do this, requires a certain know-how and demands the acquisition and use of specific skills. You must accept that it is up to you and not settle for something that is short of perfect. Incompetence, meaning unacceptable levels of performance, should not be tolerated in yourself or those you are working with. Instead, you must hone the ability to break the task down into smaller steps and appropriate guidance needs to be provided as required, to the athlete for improving performance.

It is equally important for coaches to be consistent in their performance as well. A stable mentality, remaining calm and resilient under pressure and not failing when pressure mounts are hall marks of great coaches. Apart from specialised skills, sports coaches have a responsibility to ensure that each athlete is also able to learn and take away essential life skills from each interaction they share as coach and athlete. To achieve this, coaches need to be effective, creative, adaptable, consistent and flexible but, most of all, they need to have exceptional communication skills.

This can be shown to your athlete through quantified and measurable data like match analysis, video analysis, precise and timely positive feedback and so on. In so doing, you will be anchoring words and images of progress, improvement and even high performance or excellence in the athlete's mind.

Nowadays, and I say unfortunately, success is often measured by the amount of money we earn and the number of top athletes we help develop that make it to the top. Well, I found out the hard way that that is not always true. When I trained my first high performance junior athlete I most certainly experienced exhilaration and a tremendous thrill of success. But I also found out along the way that so many of the practical skills and theoretical knowledge that seemed so important in the training manuals and during my own coach training were not quite so meaningful. They did not apply in the real live coaching sessions and I had to read across different fields and consulted some of the leading coaches in order to find the solutions I needed to help turn my athletes into high performance players. This led to my appointment to head up an independent school tennis programme and which within a couple of years was ranking among the top three coaching programmes in the county. Success and achievement cannot always be measured in terms of money.

Being a change maker essentially requires you to perfect your own act before attempting to impact other people's lives. Great coaches have no trouble getting the athlete to learn because they understand the emotional impact of their communication on the athlete as they learn. Always look for the good points and what the athlete is doing well and

Chapter 6: Long Term Self Development

commend them on this. However, it is difficult to keep learning and improving on your own. But I will show you how to reach into your resources to tap out that true potential inside of you. This is why it is important for sports coaches who wish to excel to seek mentors or guides for them, just as they are mentors for their athletes

The Guide and Mentor to the Coach

Every sports coach needs to have a mentor. This can be someone you look up to or idolise or someone who can rectify your mistakes and keep a tab on your performances. A mentor need not be someone who is particularly famous or renowned. They simply need to be someone who is able to inspire and bring about successful changes in you, the coach. In other words, choose someone who succeeds in capturing your ideas and understands what you aspire to and can encourage you with confidence.

You must take full advantage of all the professional advice and expertise available from your mentor and remember the experts in your field and truly great mentors will not come flocking to your door. They will be busy achieving their own high goals and you will have to seek them out. You will find that they will be very willing to share their knowledge and experience with you if you show a seriousness of purpose and intention to succeed. That is one of the reasons they are climbing the highest pinnacles of success and are considered as key persons of influence in their chosen fields. When you get that high, you too will find the joy and pleasure that comes from reaching out a hand or giving practical advice to less experienced coaches who are struggling as they come up behind you. As a sports coach looking to excel in your field, the decision to engage a mentor, must be given full and careful consideration.

- **Choose your mentor wisely:** Make sure the person wants the role regardless of whether they are employed as such or you are requesting this of them. A mentor who likes working with you and wants to support and see you succeed will prove to be a more positive motivating force for your professional development.

- **Time commitment:** As with any working relationship, mentoring will require a time commitment from both parties. Schedule in the necessary time and never miss an appointment without a good reason.

- **Appropriate knowledge and skills:** While the mentor does not have to be involved in the same field, they need to be or have once been involved in a similar field. This will allow them to successfully guide you and show you where the pitfalls are and effectively help prevent you from making costly mistakes in time and monetary terms.
- **Good communication tools and skills:** Meeting in person and talking face-to-face is by far the most effective form of communication and should be accommodated if at all possible. However, with the availability of advanced communication tools and technology at everyone's fingertips you can listen, see, send and receive information in a fraction of a second making good communication possible as well as efficient for both parties.
- **Good mentors are patient and supportive:** Similar to a coach/athlete relationship, this relationship is led by you the coach (mentee). The mentor's role is to guide you towards achieving your goals in the quickest and most ecological way without imposing their own views and philosophies.

Choose a mentor who is likely to make an impression on every facet of your coaching, including practical performance, relationship building with players or athletes and fellow coaches, setting examples before the team and 'being' a coach. Although I am stressing the importance of getting a mentor and gaining expert guidance, do not let them make the decisions for you. You need to cultivate the strength of character to make your own decisions and adhere to your own moral code. Either that or agree to disagree. You have to apply your knowledge to the issues in hand. Coaching is all about self-management and emerging as a true role model. It is about 'being' what your athletes want and need rather than teaching them ways to become the same! Therefore, a mentor, whom the coach himself idolises, will certainly have a crucial role to play in this.

Benefits of Having a Mentor

When you have a mentor, you have someone who can become your key source not only of support but also of unbiased advice and constructive

Chapter 6: Long Term Self Development

criticism. Here are some of the other major benefits you stand to gain when you choose to have a mentor:

- You get to learn from someone who has more experience. Since your mentor will be someone who has been where you are now and come through victorious, you know you can lean on them for wisdom. They can not only teach you the ropes, but help you recognise and overcome career challenges and see things with a different perspective.

- You have someone who can guide your career towards success. With the advice and guidance from your mentor, you can give better direction to you career and learn from their past experience about how best you can avoid the usual pitfalls.

- You get unbiased feedback and help with problems. Some problems are difficult to solve merely because we are too close to them to see clearly. This is where an unbiased third party, who has your best interests at heart plus experience in the field, can be of immense help.

- You get help clarifying your goals. It always helps to brainstorm ideas and goals with another person, especially one who has a lot of knowledge of the industry. Also, when you have someone motivating you to achieve your goals, you are more likely to follow through on them.

- A mentor can help you develop critical and creative thinking abilities. This will go a long way in bringing you success. You will learn to look at situations from different perspectives and to come up with effective solutions.

CHAPTER SUMMARY: To begin with, you need to be able to portray immense self-confidence by appreciating and understanding that you are indeed an instrument of change. You need to work on your emotional intelligence and practice controlled assertiveness in order to push your athletes or team members hard enough to challenge their limits.

- Your self-management skills should also comprise personal maintenance and upgrades, so as to remain in top form.
- You will need to impose measures, including the right diet, to maintain good health and preserve fitness levels and agility.

Are You A High Performing Coach?

- Last but certainly not least, it is crucial that you have a mentor in your life; someone who can inspire and bring about changes in you. It's all about encouragement—the best way to encourage others is to be encouraged.

 Focus on improving all areas of your life and leave nothing to chance.

Chapter 7: Managing The Body And The Mind

'Age is an issue of mind over matter. If you don't mind, it doesn't matter.'
—Mark Twain

When it comes to sports coaching, nutrition and healthcare become very important aspects of self-management. This is because sports coaching is all about training your athletes to achieve their desired fitness goals and challenge their limits. And, in order to achieve this, you are required to set an example by maintaining your own health and fitness levels. So, special care has to be taken to maintain proper nutrition, and chalk out a complete healthcare plan.

Maintaining the Right Nutrition for Coaches

Nutrition for coaches is just as important as it is for the members of your team. Good nutrition ensures that your energy levels are maintained at the high levels needed for coaching. The body needs to be well prepared to withstand the long grueling hours of physical training. You need to be able to maintain your stamina in order to encourage your team to remain on top of the game throughout the training period. Hydration is equally important, since depleting water levels could lead to low energy levels.

The diet plan should be such that it not only provides the much needed energy but also plays a crucial role in the recovery period. Just like athletes, you too, may have long days in training and are required to be in top form when you turn up for a session the following day. In most cases, there would be very little time to rest and recuperate. The dietary

norms should be adequately managed and monitored for taking care of such challenges. Weight gain needs to be kept at bay, since excess accumulation of body fat could interfere with your agility and energy levels. This is apart from leading to other health complications. Keeping all such requirements in perspective, the following nutrition tips are a useful reminder and could come in handy in addressing your fitness and nutritional needs.

Some Tips for Setting up the Right Food Habits

The way the diet of high performing coaches is managed needs to be no different from how that of a high performing sporting individual's diet is managed.

Here are some useful tips that can help coaches inculcate the right eating habits:

- Meals should be had on time. Skipping meals could cause a significant dip in blood sugar levels.
- Practice the minimum effective dose principle. Excess is not necessary.
- Ideally, meals should comprise of items that are rich in nutrients and the essential minerals, such as calcium, potassium and magnesium, yet low in useless calories. So, fat free, low oil and low carb meals should be preferred over starchy and fatty food choices that could lead to bloating and unnecessary weight gain.
- Pre-lunch and pre-dinner snacking is a must for those in physically demanding coaching practice. Snacking on healthy fruit and low calorie foods between meals is essential to keep hunger pangs at bay and ensure you receive a constant supply of energy. However, the risk is that this snacking becomes unhealthy snacking. The ideal snack items include fruits that contain plenty of water in them, oil free crackers and biscuits, whole wheat sandwiches and so on. Carbohydrate based snacks are essential in cases where the training sessions are intense and energy consuming. The timings for these snacking sessions should be fixed in relation to the rest of the diet plan and adhered to on a regular basis. While it is essential to stick to fixed meal timings, regular monitoring and adjustments according to demands of the fitness plan must be accommodated. Eating at odd times or in an unplanned manner could do more harm than good.

Chapter 7: Managing The Body And The Mind

- Foods that are high in water content need to be included in a coach's daily diet plan. Fruits and vegetables are great for water content. Plenty of fluids must also be consumed at regular intervals.

- In case specific nutrient deficiencies are detected, vitamins and supplements can be taken to make up for such deficiency. A word of warning here: make sure that a medically qualified person is consulted before vitamins and supplements are introduced in your diet.

- Fried food items or caffeine rich items, such as colas and coffee, also need to be avoided. Smoking and the consumption of alcohol should be strictly avoided to keep health destroying toxins at bay and giving your body a higher chance of functioning at optimum.

Managing the Mind

'The human mind is like a parachute, it functions best only when open.'
—John Scott

Just like managing the body, managing the mind is an equally essential aspect of successful coaching. After all, success in sports is largely about mental games and how well they can be played. Moreover, as part of your coaching profession, you also need to master mind management skills because they are required to imbibe the same in athletes and target groups. Your mind is clearly the most important aspect of yourself that you must never neglect. If you have not stopped to think about how valuable brain function is, then this may be a good time to do so.

The mind not only helps you to solve problems and handle situations you may not have encountered before, it allows you to communicate with people and understand or read information you have not come across previously. These are just basic examples. Your ability to think and process information, control of the senses and sense of awareness as well as unconscious behaviours are only possible if you are in good health. Your athletes expect a coach who is sane, clear headed, knowledgeable, able to organise, able to communicate clearly and keep the sessions enjoyable.

Are You A High Performing Coach?

Being a sports coach demands that you are able to plan your coaching sessions and come up with solutions entirely in your mind without taking any direct action. This level of human intelligence is independent of behaviour and depends on the level of understanding and amount of information you may have about the situation for which you have to plan.

Your memory retention capacity and ability to recall similar information or previous situations will allow you to come up with more than one solution to a single problem. This can help you in coaching sports groups such as tennis where each player operates individually. To be a great coach requires consistent performance physically, mentally and emotionally. You must strive to develop a serious attitude towards improving your brain function as well as a heightened ability to recognise and control emotion. A brief understanding of your own mental capabilities and knowledge of mental processes required in your sport will further enhance the quality of your sports programmes. A healthy mind is able to use one or a combination of the following skills:

- **Apathy:** While not caring is not condoned in high performing sports coaches, this note relates to not reacting to a situation or behaviour and ignoring that particular situation usually one that has no relevance to the coaching session.

- **Conscious analysis:** Ability to take in information through the five senses, acknowledge the problem and attempt to reason your way to an intelligent solution. All the while, considering potential constraints such as time, ability, physiology, relevance to the athlete and so on.

- **Instant knowing:** As an experienced sports coach, you will have developed certain skills like recognising emotions or behaviours to a point where you can do so automatically, you do not even have to think before you say or do them.

- **Data processing:** Sometimes you may not be able to help resolve a problem your athlete is having because you require more information. Your mind recognises that you do not have adequate information.

- **Multiple options:** Great sports coaches can come up with two or more possibilities or solutions to a problem an athlete may

Chapter 7: Managing The Body And The Mind

be having. These pop into your head, and you select a preferred choice from among them.

- **Suspicious or curious:** Picking up on an untruth. Perhaps an athlete claims to have trained and done all the exercises when this is not being reflected in their performance. Your mind has the ability to figure out when you are being misled. The mind automatically starts to look for the hidden information when what you expect is not met.

This information is not conclusive and is only being given to offer a partial awareness of how your mind actually works:

- **Cognitive pre-processing:** The ability to take in raw sensory input, transform it into an internal imagined representation. This may not necessarily be an accurate representation as it remains an imaginary construct in your mind.
- **Associative memory:** Ability to link or associate the internal representation to memories that may be visual, auditory, kin esthetic, emotional, or completely abstract. Allows you to recall how a similar problem or situation was resolved or improved.
- **Not applying the solution still remains an option. Without access to your memories, it would be impossible for you to solve or even to understand the problems your athletes are having.**
- **Pattern matching:** Your mind's ability to match the memory to one or more potential solutions for what may even be a completely new problem, one that has never existed in quite the same form. All athletes are individuals and unique in their performance. This is possible because your mind is able to generalise the problem and match it with a generalised solution that's already stored in your memory.
- **Expectation:** Faced with a potential solution, your mind forms expectations about what will happen if that solution is implemented. Your mind stores and processes information in general and invariant or unchanging representations. These expectations come from associated memories about what happened in the past, how the athlete performed, whether the solution worked or not. With experience, you will start to identify the desired solutions that solve the problem.

- **Learning:** The process of experiencing specific sensory input, noticing general patterns, and storing those patterns as invariant representations. This happens both consciously and unconsciously.

- **Anticipation:** The process of applying invariant representations to specific situations, so now the flow of information goes from the general to the specific.

It is important for coaches to have an all pervasive positivity in their outlook. The sporting spirit is not demonstrated in wins alone. It is also portrayed in defeats that are accepted with positivity and dignity. A positive outlook breeds encouragement. It is essential for coaches to deal with their teams with a focused mind. The mind must essentially be free from all digressions and remain glued to the goal alone!

Mind calming skills and techniques like yoga, meditation and breathing exercises need to be adopted, and practised and encouraged in your high performing athletes as well, to rid the mind of worries and unnecessary stress. It is important to maintain mental clarity and a peaceful demeanour. And, most importantly, in order to achieve the right mindset for a successful coach, all forms of negativity should be shown the door!

Additional Health Governing Tips for Sports Coaches

Apart from maintaining the right nutrition, there are several other health concerns one should keep in mind to stay in top form. Some of these include:

- **Staying happy:** It is important for a coaching professional to remain happy and enthusiastic. To stay happy, you need to manage stress, have a good work-life balance and participate in plenty of relaxing activities. Practising regular breathing exercises, indulging in relaxing activities and refraining from excess work pressure, are essential.

- **Keeping fit:** High physical fitness is the key to a positive mental attitude. It is essential to adopt the right fitness regime, suitable for your age group. You need to get your act right every time you are training your athletes or in an intense coaching session and know that you can remain fresh and energised from start to fin-

Chapter 7: Managing The Body And The Mind

ish. It allows you to think clearly and portray positive body language. Devoting a regular time to some form of fitness training is a must. Besides, regular training ensures optimum agility and flexibility both in mind and body.

- **Regular health monitoring:** Health monitoring is necessary for all sports and coaching professionals. Apart from routine checkups that ensure optimum health, regular health checks serve as a monitoring system for picking up or managing under- lying health conditions, if any. Chronic illnesses need to be managed well so that they can be kept in check. Undue disruption to the coaching schedule on account of illnesses could prove to be grossly damaging for not just the morale of the team or players you coach but that of friends, family and support network.

Coaching is about creating a whole lot of positivity in order to provide for, and create, an environment that encourages learning. It is about encouragement and enthusiasm to challenge the existing goals and scale new heights. You need to be adventurous, innovative and dynamic in your coaching session. Positive energy will spearhead this effort and needless to mention, positive energy that stems from a healthy, stress free and relaxed life.

CHAPTER SUMMARY: When it comes to sports coaching, nutrition and healthcare become very important aspects of self-management. This is because coaching is primarily about training your athletes to achieve their desired fitness goals and challenge their self-imposed limits. In order to achieve this, you must be prepared to set an example:

- By maintaining your own health and fitness levels. Special care has to be taken to maintain proper nutrition, and chalk out a complete healthcare plan.
- Good healthcare does not just mean your body, it includes your mental fitness as well. By keeping your mental skills honed, you will be a better problem solver and communicator. You will also have a deeper level of understanding of your athletes and how to effectively meet their needs.

 Make your wellbeing a priority.

Chapter 8: Business And Career Management

'When blocked or defeated in an enterprise I had much at heart, I always turned immediately to another field of work where progress looked possible, biding my time for a chance to resume the obstructed road.'
—Charles W. Eliot

Daniel Thorp is an Lawn Tennis Association (LTA) Registered Professional Coach based at Manor Park Club in Malvern. As a coach, Dan has a successful track record in many areas ranging from mini tennis to working with national level players. He works as a coach educator for the LTA, delivering the Development, Club and Performance Coach Award courses. Dan also writes as a tennis coaching specialist for the BBC online website. In 2006 Dan launched www.britishtennisparents.com in collaboration with Judy Murray and the LTA. The British Tennis Parents website provides information and advice for the parents of tennis players, to help them make the best decisions for their children. Dan's success lies in part to having excellent business and career management skills.

While health is an important aspect of being a great coach, managing your career and business are just as important. Depending on the primary motive for taking up coaching as a profession of choice, concrete measures need to be adopted so that career goals are met with certainty. Every professional aspires for success in their career. In fact, your choice of career is justified by the amount of success you achieve. Ideally, career management moves should be planned in such a way that progressive goals can be achieved sequentially.

If you aim for lucrative assignments, you should be aiming for highly paid jobs, including those granted by non-governmental organisations, and must prepare yourself accordingly. However, if job satisfaction is

Chapter 8: Business And Career Management

your primary aim, the quest is likely to be for the more challenging assignments that could require some effort for success.

Essential Career Management Tips

Some of the following tips should be considered for effective coach career planning and realising career specific goals:

- **Upgrading Skills:** Skill upgrades through effective training will keep you current and in top form for your job. Irrespective of the kind of assignment you wish to pursue, it is always necessary to remain updated with the most modern techniques and concepts concerned with sports coaching. A sports coaching professional should be able to take up challenging assignments that come his way, firstly, by qualifying for the same. Just as it is the case for most coveted professions, sports coaching too has become an immensely competitive domain. You do need to remain ambitious and be suitably trained in order to remain eligible for the most attractive opportunities that might be on offer.

- **Profile and Brand Management:** Once a professional coach is considered eligible, the next step should be to complete profile management. The profile should bear details of qualifications, training programmes and professional assignments undertaken to date. Career high points should be highlighted clearly. The profile should also elaborate your goals and professional aims and the kind of assignments that interest you. This should help with your branding which is closely linked to your name. When you or your service is requested for, the customer is making a distinct choice and wants what you can deliver. They are not looking for just any sports coach, they already know you are credible and should happily pay for your service.

- **Choosing Right:** Compromising on the choice of assignment could have a significant impact on your career. Opting for an assignment out of compulsion or compromise can throw your entire career path out of gear. Assignments need to be selected as per personal goals and aspirations. For instance, if you settle for a relatively simpler and routine assignment you may not be able to cope with more challenging assignments later on. This could be a significant loss for you if you have been looking for assignments that are specifically more exciting and stimulating.

- **Learning through experience:** Sports coaching is mostly about the practical application of knowledge and skills. Considering that it deals with relationship management and people handling, it is important to have an open mind for picking up new skills as you move from one coaching situation to the other. As you will come across different people in your coaching career, it is important to keep your faculties trained, allowing you to cultivate new skills and pick up specific human management skills to be used in future. This is precisely one of the reasons why experienced coaches clearly make a better mark than novices. These experiences are of no use to you as a professional if you do not possess the right perspective to learn from them. Whether these experiences result in successes or failure, they will continue to prove enriching in more ways than one.

- **Building the right contacts and relationships:** The results you achieve are supposed to be more than enough to speak for themselves and lead a coach to better assignments. It remains a fact that opportunities are few while the competition is cutthroat. Building relationships is likely to be of help. You need to build loyalty starting small and then growing the numbers. It is about your branding and spreading the word about the work you are doing and the kind of assignments you are interested in taking up. Public relations often prove to be a great source of assignments that you might be desperately looking for. In this Internet driven world, a returning visitor is worth a lot more to your professional success as they contribute to your efforts of building contacts and networking for mutual exchange of ideas and opportunities. Now more than ever, professionals in today's world need to bring out all their aces when it comes to building relationships.

- **Career Planning:** Irrespective of the opportunities that come your way, it is necessary to plan your career path for success. Adequate planning is required so that one assignment can logically lead to another, in the most progressive fashion possible. It is necessary to plan career moves in such a way that the career building phase can be utilised for maximum gains. No matter

Chapter 8: Business And Career Management

what the present scenario, career plans and life goals should never be compromised.

Prerequisites for Effective Career Management

Now that we have established the need to plan, the next thing is to understand that career planning requires plenty of focus, a clear perspective and considerable courage. It might not always be as simple as it sounds or perhaps appears and the very basic necessities of life, like economic stability, could drive you into making grossly inadequate choices. Con- sidering that coaching is essentially about passion and vision, compro- mises such as these could prove to be significantly damaging for your career aspirations and goals.

Plainly put, factors like economic sustenance need to be worked out first. Basic needs of life and providing the desired financial security to family members are sensitive issues that may prove to be the cause of major career compromises. At the crux of all such issues is money management. Money management or assigning of finances is an art sports coaches have to master in order to keep your mind free of allied concerns. Money management requires you to be courageous, resourceful and enterprising to ensure a safe financial outlook in which to support and promote desirable career moves.

I was really struggling to work with the head coach at one of the clubs. If I got any coaching work, it was because he couldn't make the time and I was the back-up. I had to keep turning up at the club not knowing if I was going to be allowed to work that day or not. I could not carry on like this if I was going to make a living from my profession as a tennis coach. One of the best moves I made was to decide to set up my own coaching programme.

At first I had 12 people sign up. I thought this was a good start. By the end of that month I had over 50 more sign up and the numbers were rising. I needed to get my act together and fast. I had to be organised and take care of the administration, accounts, coaching, manage the players and teams as well as keep a lot of parents happy! By doing exactly what I have laid out in this book, the programme grew to be one of the top junior tennis clubs.

Are You A High Performing Coach?

CHAPTER SUMMARY: Whatever your motivation for taking up coaching as a profession, it is imperative that you manage your finances as well as the physical and mental aspects of your well-being. Good career management requires:

- Creating goals and desired outcomes to strive for, whether those are for highly paid positions or the more challenging assignments.
- Prepare yourself accordingly by maintaining a safe financial outlook so that you can support and promote any career moves.
- Strategize your career plans with effective management by learning through experience, building contacts and building strong relationships within your community and constantly managing your brand and profile.

 Offer more value and quality service than what you are paid.

Chapter 9: Money Management

A classic example of the ideal mindset that could facilitate effective money coaching, is that of Richard Williams. Richard is credited with having taught both Venus and Serena, arguably, the two most successful sisters the game of tennis has ever had and guiding them to the pinnacle of success. The mettle of the man who coached both his daughters to the number one spot cannot be argued at any point in time. Interestingly though, Williams had never touched a racket before he and his wife Oracene caught a television commentary explaining that tennis players could actually earn thousands of dollars each week, once they achieved a desired level of proficiency in the game. That was the moment that turned his life around. It was this urge to make money that encouraged him to first learn the game himself and then coach his daughters helping them reach where they are today. Driven solely by the intention to make money, Richard Williams and his daughters achieved the impossible!

Sports coaches are known for turning the tide in their favour and lifting the morale of teams before that all important game! Therefore, it can be safely assumed that you essentially have it in you to not only motivate but swing into damage control mode when required. You are not always known to do it in many words. It is the way in which you apply yourself to your target group that makes all the difference. This is an essential quality that should make you a great money manager. Given that you have the mindset of a sports coach, which makes you effective, coaching you about money could be a cake walk!

Money Management and Coaching

With money management, you always need to assume that you are being pushed to the wall, right from the word go. Coping with tough times or wealth building will require you to react as if you are in crisis mode always. This way, it becomes easier to remain safe, enabling professionals to undertake risks for the sake of career advancements. Come to think of it, money coaching coaches is far from difficult. I believe you clearly have it in you to be a great money manager. All you need are some basic guidelines to adhere to for building the base of effective money management strategies.

Ideally, money management should feature in your list of priorities, right from the onset of your professional journey. As a professional you need to understand that planning careers according to personal preferences could mean refusing assignments until the suitable one arrives. Finances would have to be managed during the interim. This is what makes financial management, most important.

Basic Guidelines for Money Management

Some basic guidelines for money management in the sport coaching profession include:

1. **Saving Benchmark:** Remember, professionals need to have a benchmark figure when it comes to saving a percentage of what they earn. And this benchmark needs to remain in place right from the time the first payment arrives. Certainly, sports coaches should be no exception. This saving benchmark must be at least 10% of the total pay in hand. If you are not able to save 10% just yet, it should not stop you from making modest beginnings. However, the ultimate saving goal needs to be 10% or more! And the faster it is achieved, the better it is likely to be!

2. **Loan Truths:** Indeed, most of us are tempted to opt for loans; for homes, cars, consumer durables and similar such necessities of life as soon as there is a regular income of sorts at our disposal. However, it is important to exercise a high level of discretion when it comes to seeking loans. You will have to reassess your repayment capabilities and select loans accordingly. It needs to be remembered at all times that repayment of loans should never interfere with the saving schedule. Irrespective of having to pay monthly installments for settling loans, the savings amount needs to remain intact. When savings are curtailed for meeting loan demands, it becomes apparent that you have subjected yourself to loan amounts that are higher than your paying capacity. In such cases, sustaining an account that's enough for

Chapter 9: Money Management

managing risks and low income periods, could become impossible. Besides, managing high interest loans during tough times could also prove to be a problem. It is extremely important that the urge to use loans is kept in check.

3. **Investment:** Investing a portion of the saved money is just as essential as saving. It is advisable for coaching professionals to engage investment experts who can help them create interesting portfolios with constant returns. The investment plans should keep risks and income breaks in perspective so as to be of use during times of financial duress. Keeping investment plans for later could, in fact, prove to be a gross mistake. They need to be planned in parallel so that enough time can be allotted to them for accumulation of returns.

4. **Hire Purchase:** One distinct characteristic of a sports coaching career would be its unprecedented highs and lows. Therefore, it is important to keep in mind that highs may not last too long. Hence, spending aimlessly on assets or other items would have to be controlled. It is essential to resort to smart buying by making the most of discounts and offers and seeking lucrative deals that add value. Going overboard with purchases needs to be avoided at all times.

5. **Building up on Income:** Striving progressively to build up on income is always a smart move, irrespective of the type of assignments that may be of interest. Professional sports coaches must consider being part of training programmes, participating in informative forums, and upgrading of skills in whichever way possible. Create value for your athletes by offering benefits such as memberships, new services and or packages. Know how to set your fees and charge based on the value of the service you provide. This may require you to educate your current customer from time based fees. Being a professional coach who strives to remain acquainted with modern codes of coaching will increase the likelihood of landing well-paying assignments easily.

The importance of money management lies solely in the fact that at the end of the day, it will make you more confident, secure and most importantly free! This emancipation from worldly worries could, in fact, go a long way in making you a great professional who has undertaken your fair share of risks.

CHAPTER SUMMARY: Effective money management should be an important goal that you set at the very beginning of your journey towards becoming a high performing coach.

- It involves educating yourself on basic financial guidelines so that you can build up your income
- Learn how to invest your money wisely
- Good money management will provide you with the freedom to concentrate on what is really important—coaching!

 Make saving a habit.

Chapter 10: Injury Prevention and Health Management

One very promising career that was cut short due to sports injuries was that of Martina Hingis. At 22, she retired from professional tennis due to multiple ligament injuries. She spent 209 weeks as the world's No.1 in professional tennis and won five Grand Slam singles titles and nine doubles titles. Time magazine ranked her among the 30 Legends of Women's Tennis: Past, Present and Future'. In 2013, her name was elected to be included in the International Tennis Hall of Fame. Today, Martina Hingis is a coaching consultant at the Patrick Mouratoglou Academy, mentoring players like Daria Gavrilova, Serena Williams, Yulia Putintseva, Naomi Broadly and Sachia Vickery.

Being a coach can be trying in many ways. As has been emphasised in the previous chapter, it is absolutely essential for you to remain at the top of your profession if you wish to create the desired impact on your athletes. The task of coaching could end up becoming much more challenging not just mentally but physically as well, especially in the field of sports coaching which may require and involve specific levels concerning physical fitness.

Although you need not exhibit performances that can match up to those of the athletes you are coaching, you need to remain in good physical shape in order to set or demonstrate the right examples. Working with athletes for extended hours can often take a toll on your stamina and fitness.

Disadvantages of Physical Limitations in Sports Coaches

Physical limitations in coaches can have several disadvantages. Some of the most prominent ones include:

- When you are not physically fit to carry out your duties, you may not be in the best state of mind! This could then have an impact on your overall demeanour. Subsequently, as has been elaborated on in previous chapters, an imperfect demeanour can have a negative impact on the overall morale of the team or your athlete. There is likely to be a sense of hopelessness, anguish or seething frustration among players, due to the lack of positivity. You are viewed as a leader, driving your team on a path that leads them to their goals. Keeping healthy and fit will not only make you physically equipped but also mentally confident and psychologically prepared to set the tone for a robust surge ahead.

- Practically speaking, you need to be physically fit in order to be able to set practical examples commensurate to skills you introduce. Demonstrations from you play a crucial role in boosting the motivation levels of the team especially when they are young. It also helps in effective learning. Although some sports coaches might choose to have escorts who would work as demonstrators, it is always a better idea to try and perform on your own. After all, an athlete who looks up to you, the coach, develop strong emotional connections that helps them to perform with renewed gusto every time a failure is confronted.

- Considering that more often than not, you are the driving force behind the training regimes or sports programmes, any health issues encountered by you could lead to unwarranted disruptions. If you become sick too often, it becomes difficult to build a training rhythm for sustained improvements. If, as sometimes happens, you fall ill or are injured when there is a match or a competition ahead, this could lead to significant time loss.

It is important to appreciate just how much success in a sports coaching profession depends on the professional coach maintaining their health and preserving fitness levels. You need to ensure that training schedules are being adhered to, and personal health issues are not leading to unwarranted compromises at work. Being healthy and injury free will also enable you to remain in the best of moods, preparing you to cast a spell of encouragement and positivity on those in your charge. Successfully managing your own health is indeed an asset and serves as a primary prerequisite of your target group's success.

Chapter 10: Injury Prevention and Health Management

Basic Health Management for Coaches

Basic health management in sports coaches is certainly important considering the fact that you may need to physically exert yourself on a regular basis. Regular evaluation by a doctor or a physician is essential for unraveling underlying health conditions and keeping them in check. For example, if a coaching professional suffers from chronic ailments like congenital heart disorders, thickening of the arterial walls, high blood pressure or diabetes, regular medication and continual check-ups are required for keeping their health in optimum condition. Also, doctors will provide special directives in respect of the extent to which physical exertion can be undertaken in such cases. The same needs to be abided by in order to avoid emergencies. For instance, lack of calcium could lead to weakened bones and cause easy injuries that might take long to heal. Such facts can be easily detected by routine blood tests and supplements can be taken for replenishing the desired levels, reducing the chances of frequent injuries.

Periodic fitness tests are advisable for sports coaches in order to adjudge your personal stamina levels. Fitness evaluations as are required of your athletes will specify the levels to which you can stretch yourself without causing undue stress to your bones and muscles.

Above all, it is important for you to realise your limitations and practice periodisation just as you would probably advise your target groups to do. Periodisation is a process that helps sports professionals to slowly and steadily increase their physical training load, providing the required time for the body to relax and repair. Practicing periodisation is advisable as a way for planning what is required to sustain the levels of fitness in line with the demands of your coaching role. Trying to achieve too much, all at once, could prove to be grossly detrimental.

Some Specific Sports Related Injuries and their Management

One of the mandatory areas of study for part of the coaching qualification course was biomechanics and its implications to athletic performance and sporting injuries. So, when the opportunity to work in rehabilitation and physiotherapy arose I took it. I gained a working knowledge of biomechanics, rehabilitation and physiotherapy from the best physiotherapists and orthopedic consultants at the top in their field.

It is essential to have a working knowledge of sport biomechanics and its implication in your specific sport. Knowing how the laws of mechanics and physics apply to human performance will give you a greater understanding of world class athletic performance using modeling, simulation and measurement which you can apply to yourself in the process of mastering elements of your sport. It is also necessary to have a good understanding of how physical principles such as motion, resistance, momentum and friction play a part in sport performance. You need to observe correct technique and safe playing postures and use safety equipment and protective gear as recommended in order to keep any injuries no matter how minor at bay. Some such injuries and preventions for avoiding them are discussed below:

- **ACL and PCL Injury:** The Anterior Cruciate Ligament (ACL) and the Posterior Cruciate Ligament (PCL). Both these ligaments work together to provide the desired strength to the knee area. Knee strength is extremely important in most sports involving speed of movement and sudden changes of direction such as soccer and tennis. Common injuries to these ligaments are sprains. However, partial as well as complete tears in the ligament may also occur, when the player changes direction suddenly and twists his body while keeping the feet static in the present position. Sometimes, landing from a jump could also cause significant damage to these knee ligaments.

Some common precautions to be undertaken for avoiding ACL and PCL injuries would include:

- Avoiding positions that require extended loading of the knee joint.
- Building up on the strength and flexibility of the surrounding muscles and ligaments as much as possible.
- Increasing awareness of the position of the joint and body.
- Include plyometric exercises as part of your regular training.
- **Concussion:** This is a potentially serious condition whose symptoms can surface immediately or after time has elapsed. Early

Chapter 10: Injury Prevention and Health Management

symptoms could include confusion coupled with a ringing buzz in the ears, headache, dizziness, vision changes and nausea leading to vomiting. Subsequently, patients could develop poor concentration, sleep apnea, personality alterations, irritability and general fatigue. You need to seek medical evaluation immediately if you experience similar symptoms at any time. As a rule, all sports in which there is a likelihood of suffering a head injury minor or otherwise have a regulation that requires wearing protective head gear. This is to ensure that the head is protected against injuries. Although a study published in the British Medical Journal in May 2013 regarding cycle helmets and a report by Virginia Tech Center for Injury Biomechanics, have recently found that wearing head gear and gum shields do not necessarily prevent athletes from suffering from concussion it remains advisable that protective head gear be worn. Research is being undertaken to unravel the other facets of the illness so that preventive measures can be undertaken accordingly.

- **Heat Illness:** Heat illness stems from the inability of the body to dissipate heat. There are a spectrum of illnesses in this category, with heat stroke being the most severe. Therefore, you need to adopt ways for managing it well. Excessive heat could also result in muscle cramps, pulls and so on, due to lack of essential salts which can be especially painful. You need to optimise hydration strategies, prior to, during and after the training sessions.

The training and fitness regime for you and your athletes or team needs to:

- Allow enough time for ample recovery.
- Use clothing made from light or thin fabric suitable for summer weather.
- Always allow time for acclimatising to the given climatic conditions.
- Modify the intensity of the training programme keeping the prevailing weather conditions in mind.

Other common health problems coaches need to steer clear of include skin or food allergies, and fractures. However, adhering to some simple, practical guidelines could help in averting injuries and aid prompt recovery. What follows is a list of guidelines for helping to maintain a healthy and injury free sports coaching lifestyle.

- To begin with, it is essential to stick to a fitness regime that helps condition the body to build endurance and muscle strength over a period of time. It must be a gradual process.
- Every training session must be accompanied by a warming up and a cooling down period comprising of exercises for improving flexibility and must be relevant to the sport about to be performed or just completed.
- Use of protective gear and proper clothing is a must. Make sure the clothes are airy and comfortable, helping in effective heat dissipation or protection from extreme temperatures. Also, you need to ensure that protective gear is worn in the proper manner.
- Eating a well-balanced meal is advisable at all times. Here again, you need to consult your doctor and secure a diet chart that is suitable for you if you are unclear about your nutritional requirements.
- Tank up on water and fluids as much as possible especially when working in high temperature climates or weather conditions. Remaining hydrated will not only help in averting problems associated with dehydration but will also help in maintaining high levels of concentration and keeping infection at bay.
- First aid training must always be current and appropriate equipment should always be kept handy for treating minor pains, sprains and cuts.
- Make sure you know where the nearest medical facility is so that they can take care of emergencies. It goes without saying that injuries, when reported and taken care of immediately, are likely to heal faster.

It is all about being proactive about health concerns and injury possibilities. Simple preventions can go a long way in effective coach health management.

CHAPTER SUMMARY: Not only do you have to be at the top of your game, but you have to ensure that your athlete is as well. This includes:

Chapter 10: Injury Prevention and Health Management

- Maintaining proper fitness for yourself, so that you always demonstrate good physical shape
- Setting good examples by eating right and keeping a healthy diet
- Educating yourself on what injuries are common and what techniques you can use to prevent future injuries

 Book your next full medical and dental health checkup.

Chapter 11: Why Should Coaches Practice What They Preach?

'I can't play being mad. I go out there and have fun. It's a game, and that's how I am going to treat it.'

—Ken Griffey Jr.

How Lennart Bergelin Transformed Bjorn Borg

Of course, Bjorn Borg was a true legend and we all know that! In fact, it would be strange to think that the Bjorn we all know did not actually start out as a calm emotional flat liner! Quite interestingly, he was more of a spitting image of John McEnroe in every possible way! So, he spat and raged, used bad language and threw away rackets on court, damaging them rampantly in frustration. However, it was not this kind of unstable temperament that won him 11 grand slam titles in a straight row! It was the classic intervention of Lennart Bergelin that helped do the trick for him.

Bergelin possessed a calm temperament and this is what he gave to Borg, for sustained success. Or else, he would have been just another tennis hot head! Bergelin would remain as close to Borg as possible, even going to the extent of taking a hotel room right next to his. Just as balanced as he was, his main job was to keep the passionate spirit of Borg in check whenever he was on court. He had a positive, jolly temperament which helped the great Bjorn Borg to battle his nervous energies and remain stable. Speaking about Bergelin, Borg once said, 'We were like father and son. Lennart always got me in a good mood and that was certainly a big thing.'

Coaches could easily get away with any form of behaviour when they are on a winning spree. With results in your favour, literally nobody questions you. However, coaching is not only about winning. It is also about managing defeats and keeping the morale of the team or indi-

Chapter 11: Why Should Coaches Practice What They Preach?

vidual soaring during lows. If you have done your work right, these individuals will keep working on themselves long after your programme with them ends.

The Deduction

The above is a clear case of how preferences for coaching professionals, is indeed undergoing a paradigm shift. Today, the manner in which coaches conduct themselves has become as important as their professional skills and experience. Therefore, 'being' has become much more important than 'instructing'. In this liberated and free willed world of today, instructional modes of education would hardly work. Coaches should always look to lead by example. It is absolutely important to live by a set of high value standards. There is no point in having a coach who is always stressed and mismanaged to educate his team on positivity and relaxation. When team members cannot relate to the coach, they are not likely to pick up essential skills relevant for success. This is why self-management skills need to be mastered so that coaching professionals can actually remain in the best of form, both physically and mentally, setting the right examples for effective learning. They should also be able to emerge as true representatives of their sport, profession or team, reflecting their thoughts and state of mind, perfectly.

Personal Trainers: A Classic Example!

Can a portly, unfit person be a successful personal fitness trainer? Would you hire a coach that eats junk food and slouches when walking? Would you trust the information they were giving you on how to control food cravings and challenging your fitness limits to attain a chiseled physique? Well, why not? The person may actually be an excellent speaker blessed with eloquence and might also possess the required qualifications and experiences required for becoming a personal trainer!

However, what would make them grossly inappropriate for the role is the very fact that they do not 'look' or 'behave' like a personal trainer. The ones being coached have no reason to believe! Studies and have shown that an opinion of someone is made within the first seven seconds of meeting. That first impression will affect how you are perceived until you do or say something else to convince and change that initial impression. So, whatever this trainer or coach says will seem 'far-fetched' and 'unreal'. Quite naturally, students are not likely to be motivated by this trainer for achieving the same. Conversely, a fit and slim personal trainer who sticks to healthy habits himself would seem like a believable coach! They need not be perfect or the best in their domain, but should be fit enough to demonstrate that they indeed practice what they preach. And personal demeanour must essentially be backed up by a proper coaching qualification or certification and plenty of experience.

Apart from looking the part, high performance sports coaching demands that you have the ability to capture the mindset of the athlete or target teams and the challenges they might be undergoing at the time of coaching. Granted, if you are a fitness trainer or coach who has been through the trials and tribulations of aiming for that perfect body, you will have first-hand knowledge of the experience and be able to comprehend the challenges involved in achieving the same. And, you will certainly be well placed to offer suggestions that are realistic and hence, certainly more acceptable in nature. You do, however, have to be able to impart that knowledge in a way that will enable others to learn. This in turn, succeeds in making you the coach compassionate and popular. You must bear the right appearance and practice the desirable lifestyle apart from being experienced and trained adequately, for undertaking the challenges of coaching.

Coaching and Personal Performance: Understanding the Correlation

We have been emphasising the importance of coaches practising what they preach.

However, practising and excelling are not always the same thing. Excellence in sport is not necessarily a prerequisite for becoming a coach. Personal performances and those achieved by any athletes you coach are not directly related and should not therefore be judged against one another. It is perfectly possible to be a good coach without having excelled in your chosen sport.

A classic example in this realm is that of Nick Bolletieri. At 80 years of age, when his fitness is certainly not at its prime, Bolletieri is still part of

Chapter 11: Why Should Coaches Practice What They Preach?

a tennis boarding school. His status in the tennis world has been legendary. He has something to do with as many as 10 players who have made it to the number one slot including Boris Becker, Jim Courier, Monica Seles, Martina Hingis, Venus and Serena Williams, Jelena Jankovic and Maria Sharapova. Speaking about his coaching style, Bolletieri once commented, 'I really don't know fancy expressions. What I know is how to relate to people in a manner that fits into who they are. That's my thing.'

Being a successful coach is not essentially about personal prowess. It is about communicating with and educating target groups about the subtle nuances of training for yielding improvement in performances. Sports professionals who have recently tasted the flavour of success are not necessarily the best choices to become successful coaches. They may be 'hero worshipped' but perceiving them as a coach could be a gross mistake. Personal success and coaching abilities should never be confused with one another.

Refresher Courses for Skill Enhancement: The Need of the Hour

Sports coaches are also required to keep their skill sets upgraded in order to remain licensed or registered. It also helps them remain on the same page as their athletes as they too make progress. For instance, technology based upgrades like the computerised scoring patterns and digital and media technology for performance analysis should be well understood with the help of course studies, tutorials and refresher courses. Athletes will appreciate you much more if you can relate to them in the language or style of learning they are familiar with.

One of the major benefits of taking refresher programmes for the coach is to keep pace with modern day concepts. Not only does this knowledge make you feel much more confident, it also improves the quality, increases the value and generates a whole lot of respect for the service you offer as a sports coach. Often, sports coaching professionals may be excellent in their craft and instructional skills, however, not keeping track of the modern aspects introduced in the game may end up making the once upon a time state of the art coaching methods less reliable.

Are You A High Performing Coach?

Walking the Talk: The Ideal Route

'It's testimony to the longevity I've had in the game. I've had my ups and downs but I've stuck it out.'

—Brian Lara

One coach Great Britain has been eagerly waiting to see prove himself is Ivan Lendl. An exemplary sportsman and the World No. 1 of professional tennis in the 1980s, Lendl had achieved a lot during his tennis career. On 31 December, 2011, Lendl took on coaching Andy Murray. Murray had a similar initial graph to that of Lendl, having lost his first four attempts at the Grand Slam finals. All this changed when Lendl took the reins. Within a few months, Andy Murray reached the Wimbledon final and soon after won Olympic gold and his first Grand Slam victory in the US Open in 2012. He then went on to win the ATP AEGON Championships June 2013. Having achieved all this in months as opposed to years of coaching, expectations were high for Lendl as coach. In July 2013, Andy Murray became a Wimbledon Champion, achieving an historic victory that many British male tennis players have failed to do for the past 77 years. In front of a capacity crowd, and with an international television audience watching, Murray dedicated his win to his coach and mentor, Ivan Lendl. "This is especially for Ivan as well because I know he did everything to try to win this when he was playing, and I'm glad I was able to help him out when he was coaching." Murray goes on to thank Lendl for his patience and extremely hard work while acknowledging the he (Murray) is not always the easiest player to work with sometimes.

A prime prerequisite of excelling in a coaching assignment is to assume responsibility for your athlete's performance and development as well as your own. It is much simpler than most coaches consider it to be.

Simply put, it means caring, about what you say and do. Meaning what you say and doing what you say you will do. It is about commitment and doing what it takes to get the work done no matter what it costs in time, energy and effort. You are going to push through. With this attitude, success is inevitable.

Following this route will translate into you knowing your athletes as individuals. You need to always take into account (and have a basic

Chapter 11: Why Should Coaches Practice What They Preach?

understanding of) all aspects of the athlete's life that may affect their performance levels, in order to bring out the best in them. This is not just about or specific to physical performance level. It has already been acknowledged that a basic level of expertise on technical performance should be just about enough to get you started on the road to excellence.

It is your own performance and personal development as a coach that needs to stand up to scrutiny if you are to be of significant help to those you coach. Once this initial essential step of acknowledging responsibility has been taken, you can get on with developing this mentality so that it becomes a lifestyle as natural and spontaneous as breathing.

Fortunately, having a sports background, participating in competitive sport as well as training to become a coach predisposes you to learning and or developing the right attitude and personality traits.

> *'Do not judge me by my successes, judge me by how many times I fell down and got back up again.'*
> —Nelson Mandela

One day, I received a letter informing me that I could no longer use the six tennis court leisure centre facility I was using for coaching and had effectively two weeks to clear out. I was expected to leave the whole coaching programme intact. I spent the next few days in mental turmoil as I tried to find out the reason for this decision. More importantly, what was I going to do with 160 juniors whose parents had signed them up for a 12 month coaching programme with nine months still left to go?

The temptation to feel sorry for myself about the sheer injustice of this decision was tremendous.

With no suitable facility within 25 miles available to move the programme to there was nothing left for it but to write to all my clients and let them know. At first, the parents realised that I was no longer going to be the coach and complained. Then, to my amazement, I was approached by a large number of them, each insisting that they were prepared to remain my customers and drive 30 miles if that was what it would take for their children to continue having me as their coach. A few days later I decided to hire the only available venue with one court eight miles away. From the six court venue this capacity was nowhere near what I actually needed but the coaching programme needed to go on, besides I had a list of customers to serve.

Pretty soon, with earlier starts and later finishes and a few tweaks, the programme was up and running.

As much as I would like to think my mental toughness and perseverance helped me keep going, I know I could not have done it without the children who insisted I continue being their coach. As the weeks went by I found my customers' loyalty to me humbling. What they did was amazing. The majority chose not to continue with the new coach.

Every now and again, life will throw you a challenging curve ball and sometimes more than one at once. The trick to handling these situations is not to focus on you and give up. Think of those who depend on you to show up and you will find the reason to keep going. Use each of your troubles and challenges as stepping-stones.

Winning coaches like, and constantly go for, higher challenges despite the emotional trauma and financial hardships or physical pressures. This builds up the psychological strength to persevere. The last thing you want to do is let down your athletes or yourself and those around you.

Just think how valuable these emotional assets are to you personally. Consider the sweeping influence they have on your performance and quality of life. And then consider how rewarding it is to instil these same qualities in the athletes or individuals you coach.

Integrating these attributes in your coaching sessions will undoubtedly position you above the generally accepted mediocre standards of coaching. Also think about the groups you belong to or relationships you have and notice the level at which these qualities are practised. I believe part of the reason these attributes are not generally included in standard sports coaching manuals is because these attributes cannot be measured or counted.

With so many choices and activities out there competing for athlete's attention, it makes retaining players in programmes challenging, compounded by the prohibiting expense of indoor facilities that would otherwise guarantee training all year round for most sports. The fluctuating

Chapter 11: Why Should Coaches Practice What They Preach?

state of the economy tends to affect people's commitment to long-term programmes and they will often opt for the short-term more entertaining 'sport activities' rather than long-term athlete development programmes. Some of the less effective solutions include making sessions more engaging, good communication skills and understanding your athletes. More effective solutions include better child friendly sports facilities, curriculum sports programmes and access to high quality coaching courses.

A lot of sports coaches in the industry focus or place too much emphasis on the results and not enough on the coaching process to the detriment of performance in their athletes. The secret to progression lies in the principles of training. We need to focus on the hidden drivers of performance if we want to achieve better results. It is also hard to find coaches, who make meaningful efforts aimed at developing themselves in this regard and committing to scaling the tall order.

For example, if you expect your athletes to be open about acknowledging their mistakes, you need to do the same as well. You are, after all, human too. You can, and do, make several mistakes and should have the courage and honesty to own up and seek suitable damage control measures. Preparation and planning are essential but must not be so rigid and inflexible that you cannot adapt and adjust when you realise that you have made mistakes. You must be prepared to readjust as quickly as possible. It will save you time, energy, frustration and ultimately possible failure. Learn from others. Similarly, if you instruct your team to remain in shape, you must also be proactive in losing excess weight in order to set a good example.

Therefore, it is extremely important for you to 'be' what you are being perceived as. It is more about applying our own innate skills intuition and the high value standards you stand for than about applying technical knowledge or experience.

CHAPTER SUMMARY: While it may be true that coaches can get away with any form of behaviour when they find themselves winning, the truth is the only way to really see consistent results is to coach effectively. The key is to walk the walk, not just talk the talk. Coaching is more than just winning. Those who are high performance coaches set themselves apart by molding and developing athletes who continue to work on improving their game long after they have left your programme. It is about coaching through the defeats and the struggles that allows both the coach and athlete to soar.

 Identify which attributes on my list of unmeasureables you have not mastered yet and start working on it right away.

Chapter 12: Current Trends In The Coaching Industry–The New Way And Reality

The nature of sport in the world is changing at a dramatic pace. From athletic ability to advances in the technology used to produce high-end sports equipment that enhances performance. The 21st century has indeed heralded a revolution of sorts that has been driven by professionals seeking fresh avenues for achieving that coveted competitive advantage. The recent phenomenal performances and athletic ability of people like Rafael Nadal, Roger Federer and Serena Williams for example has triggered a new wave of highly advanced research into how the human brain functions in an attempt to uncover the mind's role in athletic performance. However, the way in which the game of tennis or how athletics is taught has largely remained the same, although newer trends are slowly emerging here as well. This change promises to be equally dramatic. There is more information readily available to both the coach and the athlete.

The demand for excellence is on the rise, now more than ever. Today's coaching professionals require much more to excel than just practical knowledge and experience. It is now a basic requirement for them to accomplish a deeper understanding of the sport and, more importantly, of how people learn. The transformation has not only been brought about in what is being taught, but also in how it is being taught.

And this brand new coaching pattern uses four primary pillars as the foundation. They are:

- Using a hollistic approach for developing athletes.
- Leading by example and practicing what you preach.
- Teaching in a way that is natural and learner centered.
- Adopting a game based approach to coaching.

All these four areas have to be explored by coaches who wish to excel in their profession. They need to begin by getting their lives in order so that they can successfully lead and transform others' lives. As has been emphasised time and again in this book, it is important for coaches to groom themselves as role models. Coupled with self-grooming initiatives, it would also be essential to keep up with the modern technology based concepts relevant to sports coaching. Periodic training is unavoidable. And of course, coaches must also be able to master essential people management skills and motivating players to challenge their limits in the quest for excellence.

The new trends in the field of sports coaching are about being what the target group aspires to become and promoting holistic developments in the most learner centric way possible. Sport coaching is essentially a practical art based on tried and tested, as well as scientifically proven, methods. It now demands that we be more self-aware and as we continue in our role as guides to help athletes transcend performance boundaries.

What Can Outstanding Coaches Accomplish?

A coach becomes outstanding through giving his all to every single assignment, continuously learning and developing his craft so that others can benefit from his wisdom and experience.

One who merely 'works' as a coach can never achieve spectacular results. Coaching is never about wins and losses alone. It is about creating champions in sport as well as life, who exhibit the right kind of skills, coupled with the most suited on field temperament and excellent fitness. It's about being the positive difference, creating legends and living successes and not achievers alone!

Brad Gilbert: An Outstanding Accomplisher

Apart from having a crucial role to play in transforming Andre Agassi into the legend that he is today, Brad is also the author of the famed publication Winning Ugly which is the most referenced manual for tennis coaching to date. His role became most apparent in the 1999 final of the French Open when Agassi was going down by two sets before an interim rain delay. However, after the break, Andre came back furiously into the match, defeating Andrei Medvedev to win the title!

It was all about picking himself up and challenging his limits, with all the required assistance from his outstanding coach! Agassi once commented, 'Brad taught me how to play tennis – period. He made me understand that you can hit the ball great, but if you don't play smart you are useless out there. I didn't utilise my game and Brad taught me how to do that.'

He was a coach par excellence, who had the ability to influence the very character of a stalwart like Agassi, channelling his prowess to win one grand slam after another! That is what an outstanding coach accomplishes during the course of their career; that which is way beyond wins and losses. The depth of his experiences were so great that he chose to write them down in a publication that would prove to be of benefit to coaches who aim to create tennis legends just like he did. This is probably what 'being' a coach is all about!

Bob Brett: An Outstanding Legend Creator

Bob Brett, an Australian by birth who also runs a tennis academy in Italy, created legends like Goran Ivanisevic and Boris Becker. He also coached Marin Cilic, Mario Ancic and Andrei Medvedev. Bob was always governed by extremist views when it came to creating tennis legends. In his words, 'A champion is someone who maximises his potential, not someone who has the world number one ranking. A champion has the ability to compete and bring his best performance at the biggest moment, to dig in when things are the most difficult and to beat the odds, whether personal or in your game. And lastly, loyalty. Loyalty to yourself, your career, your coach, your family. That is a champion.' Therefore, more than sports specific achievements, Brett talks of holistic enhancements here. And this is something that only an outstanding coach, who leads essentially by example, can hope to accomplish.

Are You A High Performing Coach?
How Will This Book Help Coaches to Transform Their Lives?

This book has been written to set a perspective about coaching. Now that sports coaching in the modern era essentially has a lot to do with 'being' and 'setting examples' rather than 'teaching' or 'instructing', the book provides some workable tips on self-management that are surely to be of great assistance. Be it managing, maintaining and improving career prospects or fitness levels, this book discusses some insightful pointers that can truly make a significant difference. It also provides comprehensive guidance on career management, the application of which will lead to you providing a better service, serving your customers better and increased profit. With injury prevention nutrition guidelines you are better able to maintain your physical health for better image higher energy levels, high mental health for increased productivity, creativity and innovation and stable emotional health for clarity, maintaining good relationships and ability to solve problems.

Besides, it also helps in building up on the identity and image of an outstanding coach, what he is, and what he must aspire to become in years to come. Coaching, as a concept, has been discussed in its various facets as well. This book deals with the essential qualities a coach needs to possess and the ones he should progressively acquire in order to provide a superior service for sustained results. The entire content has been liberally punctuated with stellar examples and cases that work towards clarifying concepts and views.

In a nutshell, this book provides some truly groundbreaking concepts that can be adopted for transforming the career paths of coaching professionals for the better. The book is essentially about transforming sports coaches into successful lifetime coaches, those who can build careers and not winning strategies for matches alone! It is about keeping the complete learner in perspective instead of getting entangled in wins and losses which detract attention and focus from the end result. And this is why the book aims at transforming the concept of coaching into a holistic one. It motivates professional coaches to put their lives in order and acquire life skills as well as professional skills in order to emerge as role models who can spearhead comprehensive changes that make achievers into legends.

Chapter 12: Current Trends In The Coaching Industry

What Are the Biggest Obstacles to Being an Outstanding Coach?

'The spirit of sports gives each of us who participate an opportunity to be creative. Sports know no sex, age, race or religion. Sports give us all the ability to test ourselves mentally, physically and emotionally in a way no other aspect of life can. For many of us who struggle with 'fitting in' or our identity – sports gives us our first face of confidence. That first bit of confidence can be a gateway to many other great things!'
—Dan O'Brien

Building a reputation as a coach of excellence may not be done in a matter of one season or two. It needs to be patiently and carefully constructed over time. Outstanding coaches, bring about positive changes starting with themselves, to be able to stand true to the qualities and virtues a coach imbibes. The path for achieving excellence is not always easy and may often feel as though it is full of obstacles.

For instance, self-management which has been emphasised as an essential task for excelling in the coaching profession may not be as simple as it sounds. Be it, personal fitness, injury prevention, money management or career management, these are not skills one accomplishes in one day and suddenly it is there. Bringing about permanent changes in lifestyles requires continual and sustained efforts. It is acknowledged that quitting past practices and doing away with harmful lifestyle choices could come with a great deal of pain.

Obstacles that could prove to be significant hindrances in imbibing the essential qualities the book speaks about include:

1. The level of dedication required and exerting of oneself to become a great coach is incredibly demanding. It is better to put this effort in creating better players instead! That automatically makes you a successful and dependable coach.
2. Unconscious habits such as talking too much could pose major challenges in coaching. Often, coaches feel that they are indeed providing well-meaning advice. However, for the player who needs to excel in his game on the field, the address could seem

gibberish and unnecessary. Therefore, instructions need to be short and set off with practical demonstrations.
3. Not being able to perceive oneself as a capable and professional life coach is another serious hurdle to the path of excellence.
4. Looking for short-term goals and getting entangled in qualifiable results like the number of wins and losses is equally detrimental. Just as the book emphasises, you may have winners but not great sportsmen or legends for sustained success.
5. Undertaking coaching as a project is another serious mistake.
6. Sports coaching is never just an assignment. It is about the relationship you share with your athletes and team members. Ideal coaches can sometimes be viewed like parents, in the most ideal cases.
7. Owning results may not be proper either. Remember, a coach is the guide, not the performer. Therefore, be it a win or a loss, claiming complete responsibility for it is never justified.

These are just some of the most basic flaws or mistakes one could commit as a coach that could create major obstacles in his path to excellence. The book's guidance will have a great role to play in transforming coaching careers for scaling new heights of success.

What Does a Coach Need to Set Off on this Transformational Journey?

Once you have internalised the suggestions, tips and stories in this book, the best thing to do is to chart out a course that needs to be pursued for the same. The ideal sequence could be:

1. **Decide:** The first step is to make a quality decision. Here, the goal must be to emerge as a coaching professional committed to bring about holistic improvements in target groups by setting examples and 'being' the transformational kind of coach.
2. **Training, development and skill management:** This cannot be overemphasised enough. It is essential to maintain a programme of study and personal development for continual skill enhancement and enrichment. Back-dated coaching methods and programmes would certainly fail to make a mark! Skill inadequacies should also be made up for. As with any profession,

Chapter 12: Current Trends In The Coaching Industry

there are skills and tools for the trade. Learn to use computers, action plans, budgets, machinery and equipment, techniques or methods. High performance coaching demands that you not only know about them but must be able to use them expertly. You must be prepared to learn them first hand or by other people or by studying and application and you must be prepared to become an expert.

3. **Self-management and dealing with obstacles:** Self-management in terms of career, money, health and fitness are essential. Certain attitudinal flaws could create hindrances in the path of progress. Progressive efforts need to be undertaken for taking care of them. Do not let yesterday's failures affect today's actions or condition tomorrow's hopes. Admitting shortcomings does not mean condemning yourself. With your life in order, it is much easier to keep pace with the growing demands of coaching and emerging as a role model.

4. **Engaging a mentor:** In the same way that athletes hire coaches to take them to the next level, it is important that you, the coach, have a mentor who will help you pull and monitor the different performance areas in your life. While you may have the skills to mentor others it is not always an effective strategy to mentor oneself through complex processes. As a coach and indeed as human beings we will often have blind spots that we are unable to identify or find easy to address without assistance from a second party.

It is my hope that this book will inspire you to make a start on becoming your own master coach. It touches on the six recognised basic human needs. This is about how we as humans have a need to know that we have shelter and security. Being a high level coach will increase your chances of achieving work and being able to live in comfort. The better you are at what you do the better your remuneration will be for your services and ability to provide for yourself and others.

Challenge yourself to improve by keeping a programme of study for personal improvement and spending time with friends as well as visiting different places for new and fresh experiences. This will provide the variety you need in your life to remain fresh, energised and motivated and keep boredom at bay.

Are You A High Performing Coach?

Being recognised as an expert in your field and knowing you are appreciated, will give you the tremendous sense of accomplishment that comes from being valued and respected. Through your working relationships you are able to cultivate great friendships and maintain high levels of connectedness with different types of people. Being loved by those around you helps improve your feelings of self-worth and sense of belonging.

As a highly regarded pillar of your community it is imperative that you lead by example and are able to make a difference by contributing and participating in charitable events.

CHAPTER SUMMARY: The nature of coaching is that it is always changing, ever racing to keep up with new technology and modern techniques. However, the essential keys to high performance coaching are tried and true elements that have stood the test of time. Follow the examples of noted coaches of the past and present in order to bring out the best in your game.

   Be the one people in your geographical area or virtual community, people regard as the key person in your field.

Chapter 13: How To Be A Creative And Innovative Coach

> 'A business has to be involving, it has to be fun, and it has to exercise your creative instincts.'
> —Richard Branson

According to the Oxford English dictionary, Creativity is the use of imagination or original ideas to create something. Innovation is defined as adding something new to an existing product or process so that it works better or fulfills a different need. The key skill to learn for any coach to learn in order to improve creativity is how to use the mind and brainstorm to come up with new ideas. An excellent coach is able to draw information from different sources, synthesise that knowledge and apply it in a new, concise and easy way, making it easy to teach and for others to learn. The value of informal learning acquired through personal coaching experience, books, self-development programs, shared knowledge or social interaction should not be underestimated. The learning at this level from all the varied sources is spontaneous and has no set of guidelines, rules or defined curriculum. It effectively provides a whole unconscious resource library from which to draw ideas that can be applied when solving a problem. Patience, diligence, risk-taking and creativity are clear examples of skills that cannot be measured and yet are invaluable if one is to succeed as a coach. Yet, there are no formal courses and qualifications that will teach these skills. What sets the coach that excels apart are often not just their technical abilities but also their strong personalities, high unwavering levels of integrity and positive attributes. Creative coaches work hard and are continually coming up with different ways to solve problems and bringing these ideas and processes to life through innovation and by so doing creates value.

Continuous Personal and Professional Development: Maintaining a programme of on-going study is a must if you are to remain fresh and energised, enthusiastic and up to date with current trends. Exposing yourself to new information and experiences will often spark your imagination and improve your creativity or allow you to see ideas from a new perspective. This allows you to create fresh, original or even unusual approaches of coaching or come up with new solutions to solve the same problem in different ways. Innovation does not really take place until these new creative ideas are applied to your coaching methods or implemented in your coaching programmes. The fastest growing coaching programmes are those with things that are fresh, stylish, different and new. You need to take the initiative and look to make your programmes fun and engaging.

The 9 Basic Keys To Creativity And Innovation

1. **Resilience:** The ability to take problems, difficulties, challenges, defeats, unforeseen changes and hardships in your stride. Never give up when faced with a challenge. This advanced coping skill will enable you to turn adversity into opportunity, bounce back or ride the waves of upheaval in your professional and personal life.

2. **Confidence:** You need to maintain high levels of self-confidence in your ability as a coach at all times. This is a skill that can be acquired by simple processes like engaging in positive and proactive self-talk. While experiencing success with the athletes you train will go some way towards reinforcing that, what is of critical importance is the mental conversations about self-image, self-esteem and self-belief, you tend to have with yourself. We know that success develops self-assurance. This is further reinforced through our own ability to perform effectively and by being told that we are being successful by significant others such as family members, colleagues, friends and mentors. So seek to surround yourself by supportive individuals and avoid interacting with negative influences

Chapter 13: How To Be A Creative And Innovative Coach

3. **Energy Level:** Being a high performing coach demands a high level of physical and mental toughness. The nutritional and dietary requirements to maintain a high metabolism are the key to generating energy, maintaining vitality, alertness and stamina as well as strength to do work. Developing and maintaining an athlete's mindset towards diet and nutrition is the best way to achieve this.

4. **Can-Do Attitude:** Those who seek to rise to the top appear to encounter the highest number of obstacles. High achievers do not let anything or anyone discourage or stop them. As a high achieving and performance oriented coach you expect the best from yourself and your athletes or teams at all times. That means procrastination has to be dropped. Procrastination will steel your time and energy, your will and ultimately all hope of success. You have to develop a habit of never putting any- thing off. Do what needs to be done immediately. Eventually, it will become a habit and a natural response to the difficulties that face you. The taste of success will spur you onwards and increases that inner yearning and drive and an unshakable belief to do and be better. High performance sports coaching is about action done with a sense of urgency and high levels of enthusiasm. A coach's ability to inspire and motivate others stems from being able to create a mental picture, a vision that those you coach buy into. You can only successfully portray this if you believe you can do it.

5. **Optimism:** Great coaches focus on success, how to win as opposed to how not to lose. Coaches that achieve really high levels of success are driven by something they can often not explain. They never give up hope and will constantly stretch themselves to the limit to get further in order to improve performance without letting doubt take root. A positive mental attitude coupled with a high level of positive determination is often all the ingredients you need to keep striving onwards and upwards.

6. **Self-discipline:** No amount of coaching or training will help you achieve results without your commitment and ability to take charge of your training and your life. You need to a have a system in place for achieving and monitoring your targets. Have the commitment to develop the programmes responsibly regardless of whether you are working for someone or for yourself. You must put in the effort and create your own opportunities to excel. Develop this disciplined culture in all areas of your life as well as your coaching sessions and programmes and you will reap the rewards of having focussed and more organised self-sufficient athletes and team members.

7. **Enjoyment:** Sports coaching as a profession encourages a positive mental attitude and an upbeat, enthusiastic personality. Being physically fit and doing a job you are passionate about leads to a sense of well-being and contentment. It is as well to remember that sport is about exercise and games and games are supposed to be fun and enjoyable. The more fun your athletes have during the training or coaching sessions the easier it is for them to learn the skills being introduced. This is because learning favours the relaxed mind. Having a pleasant personality will make you more approachable and you will find it is easier to develop and maintain good working relationships and release the creativity and potential within all your athletes. Being patient and having a good sense of humour are essential and invaluable skills you cannot do without.

8. **Competitive Spirit:** In order to excel in any sport, you have to compete and win. Coaching to excel encourages the warrior within to rise up and out do the opposition; it is what you expect in the athletes you train, always pushing to improve. Coaching at this level is about keeping going in the face of hostility or even active opposition. The aim is to always be prepared and keep honing the coaching skills required to develop athletes that are good competitors who are confident and believe that nothing or no one can stop them as long as they do not give up. High achieving coaches are not broken down by resistance and opposition. This is yet another quality your athletes will recognise in you and no doubt seek to emulate.

Chapter 13: How To Be A Creative And Innovative Coach

9. **Staying Power:** What good coaches understand and drum into their athletes is that giving up is not an option. It is the knowledge that there is no great victory without a great battle. Coaching is often perceived as a lonely profession. The emotional stamina required to stay true to the profession while working unsociable hours can sometimes be hard to sustain as it places substantial demands on the support network of family and friends. It is not always easy to get good mentors who you can turn to or call upon at all hours or can be there when you need them. So it becomes important to recognise when you do need sup- port and get it without compromising your emotional stability. The mental toughness and perseverance required to keep going when everything within you is telling you to stop is often a very tall order and few sports coaches choose to push through. It involves self-discipline and self-control. Not as temporary crisis measures but as characteristics of a new way of life and think- ing. Perseverance will help you develop this attitude.

Creativity and Innovation together are a result of all the other keys being implemented in your life

There is a lot to be said for being consistent in your sessions for the sake of routine and to ensure your athletes know what to expect. The key is not to remain the same for too long. Not breaking out of the monotony of a routine will cause you to get into a rut that may prove difficult to get out of. Experiment with your coaching methods to maintain enthusiasm and excitement. Look for current research on coaching methodology, which is constantly suggesting innovations. The most rewarding sessions will occur when you try something new that works. There will be times when you experience lessons that do not go according to plan and you may be forced to think on your feet. But the mere fact of experimenting will help generate interest not just for you but your athletes as well. As a good coach you should always be asking, "How can I do this lesson better?" or "How can I help the athlete learn this skill more effectively?" Look out for inspiration from different sources and ask, "How can that be transferred or applied to my lesson?"

One of the most useful ways to enhance your coaching skills is to work with different age groups and abilities. There is no shortage of opportunities to do this and you will quickly learn how to differentiate and adapt your coaching for different abilities. You will also learn how insights gleamed from one age group can be brought to bear on another. Another excellent way of enhancing your coaching is to invite a coach or athlete to the group or behave in a slightly unconventional way to concentrate the athlete's attention. I have done this on several occasions. For example I have:

- Taken a basketball size tennis ball to use in the warm ups
- Invited a high performance junior player to demonstrate at a beginner class
- Invited my own coach to coach my team of coaches
- Challenged the athletes to do unfamiliar activities just to inject a bit of excitement
- Organised a social outing with players and parents

Chapter 13: How To Be A Creative And Innovative Coach

Most young children love to run, just for the joy of running. However, once they reach puberty, many children stop running. Why is that? Obviously they no longer take part in play- ground games like catch or tag because they consider those childish. This poses a problem as their skill development is held back if their speed of reaction and movement are not good enough. I have come up with the idea of using various playground games to encourage as well as develop good footwork, agility, and balance. Sometimes there has been a bit of resistance from the older players who claim they cannot run. Some of them are comically bad at playing these games as they realise that they are only as good as they were when they last played them at age 7! But as they practice, in every case they get better and have great fun.

The games are familiar or easy to learn and the teenagers and well as adults do not mind doing child-like games as opposed to childish games. They then start to think about the best way to be great at the games like how to evade capture, who or what are the best targets, placement or positioning in their allocated space in regard to those around them and so on. So the next time I ask them to use their running skills, they will no longer feel self-conscience or believe they cannot do so.

I have also on occasion, invited a player with a disability to my coach training session. These include athletes who have lost limbs; who after being right handed lost their right arm or had a leg amputated. This player is presented as a person who loves to play the game. The talent he had of being a top athlete and dream of playing for his country were all taken away after being involved in an auto accident. He had to learn to play left handed while using a wheelchair. I ask the coaches (or students) to listen to this person and hear what he needed or did not need from his coach. This serves as a reminder to the coaches of the complexity of issues and backgrounds they may have to work with.

You will find that better athletes are often preoccupied with perfecting their shots. Break that routine periodically by asking the athletes to teach new players what they are particularly good at. Present the new players as total beginners who must learn how to do a new skill before the end of the session. This encourages a higher level of understanding of what is involved, the key movements and actions required to perform the skill. More importantly, an exercise like this teaches an athlete how to apply valuable skills including the 10 keys to performance listed above.

Are You A High Performing Coach?

With creativity, comes the potential for initial failure as you experiment with new ways of doing things. One of my most spectacular failures was attempting to spring a tournament on my players by not announcing the date. My intention was to keep the athletes alert and focussed in their training sessions and keep them working on improving their match play as the term went on. The planned tournament did not go ahead when all it achieved was a full blown litany of excuses as to why they could not play on that day or were not ready. Since then I have learned to inform months in advance followed by reminders leading up to the week of the competition. These are done via website and emails or text messaging. The use of technology like email and web video is one of the best ways to communicate extra information and is an effective way to take care of administration and coordinate meetings between people in different locations at little or zero cost.

Remember to make sure that the service you offer or coaching you provide suits the location and clientele. I have had the experience of not being able to offer a junior coaching programme at a certain location, despite numerous requests, all because there were no accessible toilet facilities in close proximity. Sometimes you may have to change your coaching style based on the audience. For instance, "serious fun" works well with older teenagers and showing that you trust them to learn advanced stuff and "respectful casual" with adults.

Incidentally, the fact that Tennis is so popular in Great Britain is a very good reason for not having only one coach training organisation. Having the same system in every registered coaching facility stifles development of a sport and discourages the breakthrough of highly talented and creative coaching. Discouraging trained and licensed coaches from deviating from the established and 'approved' often outdated inflexible coaching systems has not helped either.

When I first started coaching in England I would get a lot of clients who were surprised to discover that I was black African and could play tennis, let alone teach it. This was very interesting to me and it unexpectedly gave me a much fuller insight into what sort of people played tennis and why. Even though by then, I had been coaching and playing the game for years. What I also discovered was that I was living in an area where the majority of people had never seen a person of colour in real life or interacted with one. It also gave me a realisation and appreciation

Chapter 13: How To Be A Creative And Innovative Coach

of the situation I was in but had not fully put together before. That racial discrimination, something I had never really experienced before, was in these parts still alive and well. This caused me to underestimate the destructiveness and resentment that was growing among other coaches who were seeing me develop coaching programmes where there had been none. Especially, when most of these coaches were far more 'qualified than I was and considered themselves to be superior.

Once while working and coaching at one of the local sports clubs, a senior member came along and was amazed to find me coaching a group session in which his son belonged. Without so much as a glance in my direction, he called his son out of the session and they left. The rest of the players and a few parents who had witnessed the whole scene were just as bemused as I was. After the session, we all speculated about what the young lad may have done that had led to his father being upset. I, however, did not have to wait long to find out as a notice followed a week later asking me to leave the club. It turned out the senior member did not approve of a black person teaching his son and had threatened to stop being a member if the son was not assigned to another coach. Rather than risk losing this longstanding member, the chairman felt it prudent to suggest I leave instead. This became a different type of learning as well as coaching experience. Racial segregation was not a concept the children I was coaching were aware of as they struggled to understand why their friend had been stopped from playing, his father's behaviour and what it all that had to do with me stopping coaching them.

Some were immediately fascinated. However it is one thing to know it, and another to turn it into a successful teaching strategy or life lesson without causing offence.

CHAPTER SUMMARY:

- We have a tremendous opportunity to be creative and innovative in coaching. All you need is to know when, where and how to use it.

- Make certain that your innovations are relevant and support the theme of what you are coaching and match your personality and skills. You cannot in all fairness ask your athletes to do what you yourself are not prepared to participate in.

- New gimmicks and trends for their own sake are of no use. Occasionally, some entertainment is defensible but must have a connection to what you are coaching, especially if an athlete starts to depend on them. Ensure progression within the same drill, for instance.
- Learn to build anticipation within the lesson or leading up to the next lesson and allow the athlete's enjoyment of the learning to grow.
- Always look to learn and try to look beyond the conventional way of doing things.

Leading In The Dark (My Story)

In 1989, I started teaching my friends and their children how to play the game of tennis. In 1991 while living in Malawi as expatriates, we as a family joined a country club where the local Malawian children were not allowed to play or come into the club grounds unless they were coming in to work for tips. They would stand outside and watch the members playing on the tennis courts, through the wire fencing. I was crazy enough to invite a group of these children in to play on the courts. My audacious act caused an uproar, anger and panic among the members of the club. Committees and the Board of Directors claimed this was against the law and could not be allowed to continue. As they could not produce the paperwork on which such a law was written, I continued. Apart from the resident coach, they were the first indigenous Malawian children to play tennis on those club tennis courts. I was the first black female committee member. Is that all I did—launch a new tennis programme? Of course not. I risked my family being banned from the club. People avoided me (at first) because they thought I was a trouble maker. I did difficult things, such as defending the rights of the children to enjoy and experience the game, even if it meant taking full responsibility for their safety. There were many times I put myself in harm's way when the club security guards would take batons to them and

Chapter 13: How To Be A Creative And Innovative Coach

manhandle them as they got thrown off the premises. I pushed obstacles out of the way and stood my ground when push came to shove. There was only one of me at first, then three of the committee members, and then the majority. Now I insisted it be written down. The children could not pay but could keep the grounds clean and tidy and help with the court maintenance in exchange for court time on one court without being thrown off. Another condition I laid down for the children was that school was mandatory. Almost every week for 2 years I was there to make sure they got their allocated court time. Together, with a group of 24 children all highly-skilled tennis players who knew all there was to know about how to maintain and look after clay tennis court. We knew we had a job to do. During those years my job was to help these children see a different way of life and dream of a better future for themselves and others like them. All I did was lead.

 Remind yourself of what you love about your sport and your own early commitment to learning as well as coaching.

Are You A High Performing Coach?

Six Key Elements to Being A Great Coach

My favourite literary model is the one about the proverbial six friends:

Who, What, When, Why, How and Where

- **Who:** As a sports coach recognise the power you have and respect it. You have the capability to impact your athlete with the same influence as a relative or parent might have. The changes you can effect are absolutely substantial.
- **What:** A great coach does the right thing, in the right way, with the right attitude -- every time.
- **Why:** Because you care. If you don't care do something else. Your athletes will do what it takes not to let you down if they know you care about their safety.
- **When:** Now. Never stop learning whenever you can. Power is really knowing what to do with the knowledge you have. Training and education are a potent force.
- **How:** Empathy, enthusiasm and sympathy are emotions that cement the learning experience. Combine these with credibility and sincerity to validate it.
- **Where:** Any time, Anyone, Any place. Good coaches are always prepared.

The road to a transformational sports coaching career could be a long drawn one. However, going through this book and using it as a checklist, a reminder or reference for steps that need to be taken, can certainly be of help.

Are You A High Performing Coach?

'In the end, it is the extra effort that separates a winner from the second place. But winning takes a lot more than that, too. It starts with complete command of the fundamentals. Then it takes desire, determination, discipline, and self-sacrifice. And finally, it takes a great deal of love, fairness and respect for your fellow man. Put all these together, and even if you don't win, how can you lose?'

—Jesse Owens

SUGGESTED READING

Because a book has the power to change the course of your life, one word at a time.

Brendan Burchard,	*The Charge: Activating the 10 Human Drives That Make You Feel Alive* (2013)
John Whitmore,	*Coaching for Performance* (2009)
Brian Lara,	*Beating the Field: My Own Story* (1995)
W Timothy Gallwey,	*Inner Game of Tennis* (1986)
Graham Winter,	*High Performance Leadership: Creating, Leading and Living in a High Performance World* (2003)
Stephen R. Covey,	*The 7 Habits of Highly Effective People* (2004)
Richard Stengel,	*Mandela's Way*: *Lessons on Life* (2010)
Richard Branson,	*Like A Virgin: Secrets They Won't Teach You At Business School* (2013)

Acknowledgments

Coaching has been a major part of my life and it is thanks to the following people without whom I would not even be writing about it: Coaches Duncan Mtonga, Solly Patel, Max Sichula, Charles Applethwaite, Anne Pankhurst, Roy Pankhurst and Robbie Dunster.

Thank you to my tutors and mentors, Mark Tennant, Daniel Thorp, Rob Antoun, Adrian Rattenbury, Clive Nelson, Caroline Marsh, Richard J Cheetham and Louise Deeley.

Thank you to Peter, Kevin, Jonathan , Stuart–It was a genuine pleasure to work with you all.

Thank you to Alison Walker and Elizabeth Williams for all your continued friendship, support, advice and guidance over the years.

Thank you to all the thousands and thousands of people I have worked with over the years, for your belief in me and my skills and the opportunity to learn from each and every one of you.

My Personal Acknowledgements:

Huge, huge thanks to my son Michael, who continues to be the most important, positive and motivating force in my life, and for your quiet confidence and genius mind.

To my family Gregory, Paul and Steven, Susan, Stephen and friends Richard, Martin, Vicky and the late Barbara Kerridge , thank you for your patience, faith, humour and endless supply of encouragement and support and for being a part of my life.

Thank you to my mother who though no longer with us continues to be the most influential voice in my life.

About The Author

Caroline Gossage is a Tennis and Mental Skills Performance coach based in Dorset in the United Kingdom. She coaches in schools and clubs, runs charity programs in the community and exclusive programs for private clients. She has extensive knowledge of developing junior tennis athletes of all ages and ability from grassroots to international levels. She is a Senior Performance Coach and Lawn Tennis Association (LTA) Licensed with training qualifications and memberships to leading international Coaching Organisations including, PTR, ITF, RPT, USTA, ABNLP. Trained by Oscar Wegner to Level 4 in Modern Tennis Coaching Methodology and is an Inspire To Coach trained Cardio Tennis Instructor.

Caroline was the first UK black female tennis coach to be registered with the LTA and is the founder of CG Tennis Academies, a company that has developed successful tennis coaching programmes for independent schools and clubs both in the UK and abroad.

She is qualified in Neuro-Linguistic Programming for Sport Performance, Fitness Strength and Conditioning, Sport Psychology Practitioner and Life Coach. Caroline is the creator of Tennis NLP, a powerful and effective coaching system that applies NLP techniques and principles to tennis coaching to accelerate learning and achieve lasting results. She also has specific expertise in working with female athletes ranging from 8 to 20 years old.

Caroline consults with sports coaching associations and keen to help sports coaches become high achieving professionals so they can make a living and enjoy a great lifestyle from their profession.

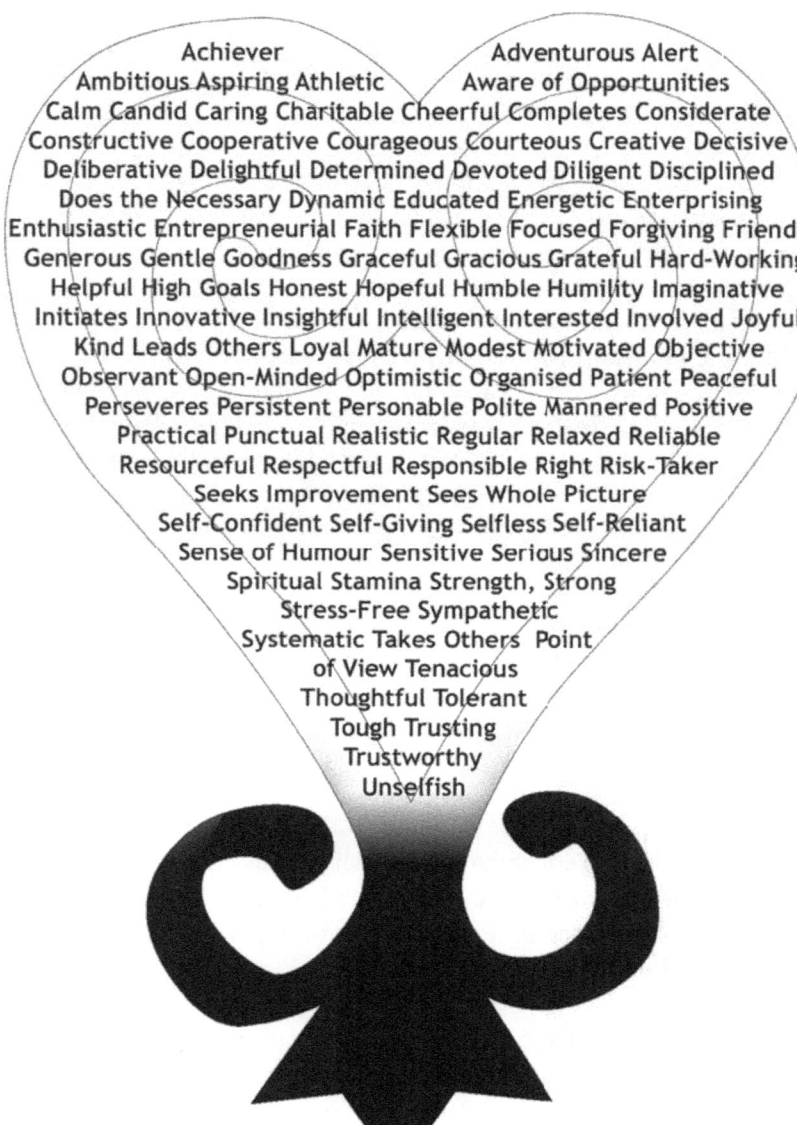

www.ingramcontent.com/pod-product-compliance
Lightning Source LLC
Chambersburg PA
CBHW032127090426
42743CB00007B/495